GAME ON: Tools and Strategies for Living on Purpose

Joseph E. Kimbrough MEng., Ed.D.

GAME ON: Tools and Strategies for Living on Purpose
Copyright © 2013 Sensible Business Consulting Group, LLC.

All rights Reserved. No part of this publication may be reproduced, stored or transmitted in any way or by any means (electronic, mechanical, photocopying, recording or otherwise) without written permission from Sensible Business Consulting Group LLC.

Disclaimers and copyright information: See reference section

ISBN: 978-1-937400-50-7
ISBN: 978-1-937400-51-4 ebook

Printed in the United States of America

Sensible Business Consulting Group
39555 Orchard Hill Place, Suite 600
Novi, Michigan 48375

Acknowledgments

This book would not have been possible without the support of many people. I would like to express my gratitude to my immediate family, Christina L. Kimbrough M.D., and my three beautiful daughters, Jasmine, Olivia and Ciara Kimbrough. And truly thankful for my parents Barbara and Eddie Kimbrough Jr. and siblings Catrina, Eddie and Tyrone.

I owe a special debt of gratitude to Charles M. Johnson II, Belinda Barnes and Brian Perkins, the talented consultants who worked tirelessly to help me develop the concepts in this book. Many thanks to the following: Pastor Solomon Kinloch Jr., Dr. NiJuanna Irby-Johnson, Renee Truitt, Valarres Bristol, Karen Ewing, Rita Chatman and many others who encouraged and supported me in completion of this project.

Thanks to Frank Cage and Caleb Davis for cover design and Darlene Carol Dickson of Manifold Grace Publishing House for book layout.

Finally, I'm thankful to God for giving me the strength and grace to overcome life challenges by producing a product that has impacted and improved the lives of many.

Table of Contents

	Acknowledgments	v
	Preface	ix
	Recommendations and Testimonials	xi
	Introduction	xv
Section 1:	The Myth of Leadership	1
Section 2:	Defining Success	15
Section 3:	Preparing for Success	31
Section 4:	Background Check	41
Section 5:	Positive Perspective	51
Section 6:	Triumph Realized	61
Section 7:	Action Planning	69
Section 8:	Time Management	81
Section 9:	Effective Communication	93
Section 10:	Motivation	103
Section 11:	Foundations of Mentorship	119
Section 12:	Conflict Management	131
Section 13:	Assert Yourself	145
Section 14:	Leading Others	157
	References	169
	About the Author	173

Preface

Think about it, how magnificent would it be if you had the skills and attitude that allowed you to realize the greatness you thought about or dreamed of? Are you America's next success story? Congratulations! However, in order to make it to the top, you will need to understand that success does not happen by chance or overnight. You have to plan and work for it. Working for it in the context of this book, requires reading and understanding the material, completing the exercises, working through difficult issues, being honest with yourself and being proud of your accomplishments. If taken seriously, this book will demonstrate that triumph comes from determination, counting up the cost and realizing that your past has nothing to do with your future.

Success begins with understanding who you are, planning and realizing your potential and prevailing over the struggles of lack of motivation and indifference with applied knowledge and the courage to be you. This book will illustrate that you can achieve, if you come to terms with the ideas that excuses are barriers that just need to be overcome and you are uniquely and wonderfully made with the ability to make the tough choices. The truth is many individuals just need to be pointed in the right direction or given a map. Think about it, how often do you take a trip without a map? Without a quality roadmap, you are joy riding with no destination. Without a destination you are wasting gas. As gas prices begin to rise, wasting gas and time will prove to be too costly.

I challenge you to read "Game On: Tools and Strategies for Living on Purpose:" take the journey to discover your true potential and be the best you can be. I am driving where you want to go; the concepts in this book are the map. Today is your day. Your pit stop is over. The rest area is closed. It's your life, take the wheel. I'll see you on the road. GAME ON!

Joseph E. Kimbrough, MEng., Ed.D.
President, Sensible Business Consulting Group, LLC

Recommendations and Testimonials

Excerpts from our clients

"Greatness can only be achieved by your willingness to follow God's divine plan no matter what...But what if you get off track? What happens if your plans get derailed? Dr. Joseph Kimbrough, president of Sensible Business Consulting Group, LLC has helped thousands of people get on target with powerful yet realistic blueprints in seminars, churches and weekly radio features. Now he's developed a book to give you that added push to walk... maybe even run into your purpose and greatness. Congratulations Joseph! "GAME ON: Tools and Strategies for Living on Purpose" is going to bless so many!

Randi Myles
Midday Host and Assistant Program Director
Praise 102.7, Radio One

~~~~~~

"Again, I wish to thank you for being such an integral part of a successful event. Each individual that we were able to reach together, left the room with more knowledge than when they entered, more confidence as they departed, and most importantly, with more hope to sustain them as they faced the next day. I am very appreciative of all you did to make the

Job Seekers Boot Camp a success and I hope you will not hesitate to call on me or my office should I be able to be of any help to you or the Sensible Business Consulting Group in the future.

With every good wish!"

Sincerely,
John D. Dingell
Member of Congress

"It is a distinct pleasure to recommend to you Sensible Business Consulting Group (SBCG). I was very pleased with the professional instructors and the manner in which they communicated the topics so that our participants could easily understand and effectively practice...I feel confident in recommending SBCG to any company or organization who wants to enhance the quality of their programs as well as provide their customers with an invaluable training experience."

Sincerely,
Tracie Lewis-Jennings, MRC
LARA-Michigan Rehabilitation Services

"It is my pleasure to recommend Sensible Business Consulting Group (SBCG) as a premier organization of innovative thinkers, problem solvers and enthusiastic facilitators. SBCG creatively introduced goal setting matrices, cause and effect diagrams and continuous improvement processes through

beneficial case studies on life and leadership...We are thrilled with the level of SBCG's craftsmanship and professionalism and look forward to retaining their services for our programs in the future."

Jason D. Lee
Executive Director, DAPCEP

"On behalf of the Education Achievement Authority of Michigan, I take this significant opportunity to express my sincere appreciation for Sensible Business Consulting Group, President Joseph Kimbrough for participation and delivering an engaging, high energy, motivational workshop on leadership at our Super Youth Leadership Summit at Michigan State University...I surely recommend Mr. Kimbrough – Motivational Speaker and President of Sensible Business Consulting Group to any other school or educational institute looking for an enhanced opportunity for its students."

Tyrone E. Winfrey, Sr.
Chief of Staff,
Education Achievement Authority

"The University of Michigan-Dearborn Gaining Early Awareness and Readiness for Undergraduate Program (GEAR UP) is a national college access program started in 1999, now in 47 states...I would like to express how pleased we are with the great work SBCG continues to provide for the University of Michigan-Dearborn... SBCG believes that by

achieving balance, students will improve math scores and demonstrate leadership traits. We are pleased that our students were led down a path whereby they were encouraged to internally make choices that will positively affect their mental and physical well-being...On behalf of the UMD-GEAR UP program, we thank SBCG for their contribution to the lives of children and highly recommend their leadership to other organizations."

Sincerely,
Perry Boyd II, Program Manager
Student Success Center
University of Michigan-Dearborn

"Dr. Joseph E. Kimbrough has been a wonderful addition to Oakland Community College (OCC) as a STEM Intervention Adjunct Professor and Seminar Instructor. He provides training and development for various degree programs, from medical to engineering, that helps students matriculate throughout OCC. He has a passion to motivate, encourage and impact the lives of individuals looking to go to the next level in their career pursuits. The training and development programs are well received and motivational to his listeners. Dr. Kimbrough's ability to take complex concepts and make them relatable to his audience allows them to enjoy his teaching while at the same time grasp a good understanding of the information being presented. Dr. Kimbrough's energy is infectious and I am proud that his labours have led to the production of this resource that will be sure to help more individuals."

Valerie Merriwether
Faculty, Academic Support Center
Oakland Community College

Introduction

Most of us, when engaged in a contest or conflict against a known opponent or enemy, can create and implement a win at all cost strategy enriched with cunning and endowed with determination. What happens when the person you are fighting is you? Will the same rules apply?

To quote Dr. Martin Luther King, "the ultimate measure of a person is not where they stand in the time of comfort and convenience, but rather, how they stand in times of challenge and controversy." The longer you live, you will be confronted with challenges and depending on your choices and how you choose to handle yourself, you may be bombarded with controversy. How will you stand? What will you do in the midst of confrontation? Will you rely on examples set by society? Will you reference role models or remembered reactions from relatives and friends? Will you conform to be popular or will you stand for what you believe? Will you make excuses?

If you do not have all of the answers, do not worry. At several points along your journey to maturity, you will question yourself. Most scholars will agree that even as adults it is only natural to revisit your values and beliefs. Why? Issues arise to challenge your moral fiber and framework. The struggle is identifying sources of strength, maintaining motivation and consistency as you advance in the face of indifference. It is the courage to admit, take responsibility for and to be accountable.

Suppose you are capable of standing, life shifts and you get knocked down, what is your plan for getting back up again? The struggle is identifying and dealing with past failure and negative experiences. The challenge is simply to begin to dream again or to overcome frustration and fear by learning to control your thoughts and to leverage your accomplishments.

We live in the information age. Just as computers have issues, we too develop glitches in our programming that become apparent in our personalities and evident in our character. Personal trials exist whether it is issues with our weight, loss of a loved one, peer pressure or the diseases of entitlement and apathy, we all have a personal struggle. For most of us the challenge is merely getting out of our own way. This struggle involves breaking free from complacency to grab something even better – greatness. Regardless of life's circumstances, our responsibility is to bridle those inner thoughts that prohibit us from reaching our potential and the goals that we set for ourselves. The capacity to reach our dreams and become our very best exists inside of us. Are you willing to persevere?

In the context of this book, perseverance requires identifying your weaknesses and capitalizing on your strengths. The key is to discover that qualities, essential to your personal achievement, can be learned, your struggle can be overcome and you can emerge triumphant. To begin, you will have to take an objective look at what you believe. Then examine your potential and unravel the foundations of the barriers to your own personal success. You will be confronted with the view that only a few special people are chosen to lead and you will have to decide whether you believe that leaders are born or made.

You will also have to examine the importance of planning, commitment to setting goals and taking action in spite of obstacles. You will assess your attitude and better understand how your past and present influences affect your decisions. You will learn that anger and fear only hinder you from doing great things. You will learn the skill of prioritization. Finally, you will realize that this struggle to lead can extend to leading others. You can continue to grow as long as you take responsibility, think ahead, and implement steps to become a better person. It has been said that anything worth having is worth fighting for. Overcome your struggle and become successful.

Section 1: The Myth of Leadership

Nature versus Nurture

Imagine you are a citizen in a small nation in the Middle East that is governed by a sovereign king who has been blessed with one son and twelve daughters. The nation is oil rich. The commerce and economic systems are subject to supply and demand. The nation has several enemies who prize its natural resources and have tried many times, unsuccessfully, to attempt a coup and seize power. The latest failed attempt sparked an insurgence as citizens attacked the king's men. This nearly plunged the country into its fourth civil war in 20 years. In retaliation, the king ordered an invasion into neighboring countries hoping to extinguish the fire of rebellion being stoked by the terrorists who hid just across the border. The king's attacks have not helped in resolving conflict but have only served to upset enemy nationalist living right in the country.

Recently on the six o'clock news, the lead story announced that terrorists were successful in assassinating the king and most of his top advisors. According to the constitution, the king's oldest male heir would assume power. In the midst of the country's grief, it occurs to you that the prince is only thirteen years old. Other than political appearances with his father, the prince has seldom been seen. Little is known about his demeanor and personality. The details surrounding the prince's education and experiences are not common knowledge, shielded by law. Added to that, the prince has five older sisters who have demonstrated competence and compassion in acts of community service and diplomacy.

In spite of national outcry and family appeals led by the king's eldest married daughter, during its emergency session parliament goes with the constitution and crowns the thirteen year-old king. Your mind starts racing. Would you entrust your family's well-being and the nation's security and stability to a child, now that the country is going to war?

During the coronation, you can't help but wonder if the prince's birthright should be the only consideration in determining the country's future. Does being born a prince mean that the person automatically has the tools necessary to be the army's top leader and strategist, the nation's diplomatic leader - be crowned a sovereign king?

What do you believe? Is it true that people are born leaders?

_____

_____

It has been said that true leaders are born not made. That must be true, right? Now, there are people who have been endowed with talent, charisma, and personality from birth. If you buy into this idea, the implication is that there is no hope for the rest of us. All we can do is stand idle, stare in awe and hold those who were "born great" in high esteem. To be average, then, means that we, the majority, will never reach our goals.

This would mean that it's not necessary for "the chosen"

to spend time on personal growth or on educating themselves, because fate has already destined them for greatness. If you believed this, personal development and education wouldn't pay-off for you since you were not blessed with the "proper" genetic building blocks, born in to the right family, or blessed with remarkable beauty – you'd have no chance at success.

While we all have been gifted from birth with unique talents, the idea that "destiny" just happens to some people is an illusion. Regardless of our gifts, none of these gifts can help people reach their potential until the skills associated with those gifts have been honed, coached and developed. Consider your favorite musical artist or athlete. Most of us would agree that because they sing or play well that they must be gifted. But, have you ever stopped to think about the countless hours of vocal and physical training necessary to consistently perform at an extremely high level.

To worship our favorites for their "natural ability" makes their success a crutch to support our failure to practice and work hard on our skills. In other words, this myth has been used by many as an excuse to not strive to be better. People feel justified in not even trying and are satisfied with mediocrity, because, in their minds, they will never be as good as the star. The first step in conquering your personal struggle is to throw out thoughts like this and realize we all have the potential to achieve great things.

Is leadership based only on a position or title?

Many think that a leader is someone with a fancy title or an important position. They think that the higher their position is or the longer their title is, the better leader that person must be. For this reason alone, many strive to gain a position of power, thinking it will bring them respect and achievement. Truthfully, what matters most is not the title or position, but the person you become. The best leaders have positive qualities that are worthy of respect and that help them to rise above challenges and adversity.

Make a list of qualities that leaders have?

_____

_____

How do these qualities help people to be good leaders?

_____

_____

Think of a person you consider to be a great leader. Concentrate on how they look and dress, their actions, routines, habits and way of life. Then, answer the following questions.

Why did you select this person?

_____

_____

_____

What qualifies this person to be a leader?

_____

_____

_____

Do you picture yourself to be like this person?

_____

_____

Why or why not?

_____

_____

Do you currently possess any of the qualities this person has?

_____

_____

When you listed the qualities of a leader, did you include:

___ Motivation   ___ Flexibility
___ Ambition   ___ Energy
___ Honesty   ___ Cognitive ability
___ Integrity   ___ Charisma
___ Self-confidence   ___ Initiative
___ Creativity   ___ Tenacity

Which of these qualities is a person born with?

_____

_____

Which of these qualities is developed over time?

_____

_____

Throughout this book you will be confronted with thoughts and ideas that will assist you in determining your own path to success. It is intended to bring out your potential to live your life successfully. Whether you are consumed with self-doubt or believe you are on the fast track to the board room, the tools in this book, if applied properly, will allow you to see the greatness within. Always remember your level of achievement begins with you and ends with you. You are the captain of your vessel, navigating your life in the direction that you intend for it to go. Staying on course, in spite of distractions, is your mission.

Consider the following examples as you begin mapping your road to success.

Walt Disney's failures and perseverance made him a success:

Like most people, you probably think of worldwide theme parks and Mickey Mouse. But he was also an Academy Award winner, film producer, screen writer, voice actor, animator, entrepreneur and philanthropist.

All of those roles can define success. But before he created the successful Walt Disney Company, which now "earns approximately $35 billion a year" (Life, n.d., p. 246). Walt Disney endured many, many failures. He started from humble beginnings, he did not inherit wealth. He had to struggle, persevere and build his enterprise from the ground up.

When he was in high school, Walt Disney took night classes at the Chicago Art Institute; he became the cartoonist for the school newspaper (Hunter, 2013). He wanted to join the U.S. Army but was rejected because he was underage. Despite his age, he was determined to serve and was able to join the Red Cross, aiding the United States overseas as an ambulance driver. When he returned to the U.S., he was not able to get a job as a cartoonist or an ambulance driver. His brother was able to get him a temporary position at a bank. When the job ended, he and a friend started a commercial art business. There were issues with the business and Disney had to leave the business temporarily to earn money to keep the business going.

While working outside of his company, he became interested in animation and found cell animation to be profitable, deciding to open his own animation company. With high employee salaries and studio costs, Disney discovered he was unable to successfully stretch the money he earned. As a result he was loaded with debt and eventually the company went bankrupt. Disney also lost the rights to a character he created named Oswald the Lucky Rabbit, it took 78 years to get the rights back for this character. After losing the rights to Oswald, Walt created Mickey Mouse (Gabler, 2007).

After the success of Mickey Mouse, Disney produced an animated feature-length version of Snow White, which was so expensive that the company ran out of money. Disney also had a hard time finding support for his dream creating Disneyland. His brother would not fund any part of the park, so Disney cashed-in his insurance policies. Media day for the park opening was the worst opening in modern times. According to Roller Coaster History (n.d.) Walt Disney's problems continued:

There were problems on opening day. The asphalt was only put down at 6:30 in the morning and, along due to the hot weather, it was sticky. The park handed out 11,000 personal invitations, but more than 28,000 people showed up - many had forged invites. Because of the large crowds and heat, almost every ride broke down. The Mark Twain riverboats overflowed with water, because there was no safety limit so the crowds piled on until the ship took on water. There was a plumber's strike so Disney had to choose restroom water or drinking water. He chose restrooms. Refreshment stands ran out of food and drink and the mayor of Anaheim, California went home, it was too chaotic at the park (para. 5). This bad opening didn't forecast the success to come!

Tyler Perry suffered for his art – and it paid off big.

Tyler Perry is an American playwright, screenwriter, actor, director of movies and stage plays. He's also a high school dropout who went back to school to earn his GED. He is quoted as saying he was "unhappy and miserable during the first 28 years of his life."

In a 2009 interview with CNN's Soledad O'Brien, Perry talked about the difficult route he walked on his road to success. Perry said he grew up in a poverty-stricken neighborhood in New Orleans with an abusive father who would routinely beat his mother and him too (O'Brien, 2009). To escape from the drama of his home life, Tyler focused all of his energy in his local church's youth group. He participated in the choir and performed in several stage plays. He enjoyed the atmosphere so much that he decided to study to become a minister. His first sermon was a flop. He could not get his message across because he made those in church laugh instead. After his sermon, the pastor of the church asked Perry to not pursue becoming a minister – he was devastated.

In 1992 Perry saved $12,000 and rented out a theater. He wrote, directed, promoted and starred in his own production. Perry's production failed; during the entire weekend run only 30 people showed up. After the show Perry was broke, broken and homeless. He was bitter and angry at God. For the next six years, he had a string of odd jobs and on occasion he lived on the streets because he could not afford to pay the rent. Still, he refused to give up on his dreams for the theater. According to Entrepreneur Voices (2011):

Then in the summer of 1998, Perry financed the

production once again. This time, he vowed, would be the last, if it failed. That production of Tyler Perry's I Know I've Been Changed opened at the House of Blues in Atlanta and sold out eight times. Two weeks later the play moved to the prestigious Fox Theater in Detroit, Michigan and sold out all 9,000 seats (True Story, 2011).

After the show, every person who had told him 'No,' every promoter who had turned him down, came to make Perry an offer. He followed "I Know I've been changed" with several other notable and successful stage plays.

The success of Perry's stage plays led him to develop a feature film. Perry took the screen play Diary of a Mad Black Woman to Hollywood and met with several prominent studio representatives. Some said his screen play would never become a movie telling him that Black people don't talk like that and that Black Christians don't go to the movies. Other executives wanted to change Perry's formula and have complete control of the story line. Perry refused, became frustrated and again contemplated placing all of his personal finances on the line to follow his dreams. Finally, an independent studio offered him the opportunity to make the film and to maintain control of creative license. The film was a success and launched several other highly profitable films. In 2008, Perry opened his own studio, where he currently produces project for the big screen as well as comedies for national and cable networks.

Answer these questions as they pertain to your future.

1. What is important to you now?
_____

_____

2. Will these things have an influence on your life later?

_____

_____

3. List your best qualities.

_____

_____

4. What would you change?

_____

_____

_____

5. What are some of your goals?

_____

_____

_____

A winning mindset starts with creating a mental picture of oneself as a leader who is working towards a goal.

Leadership Types

As you are starting to identify leadership traits in yourself, it is important to discuss the common leadership styles and their attributes. Most leaders fall into one of three types or categories. There are Encouragers, Stabilizers, and Discouragers. As you read about each, think about a person you know who fits the category.

The Encourager

The Encourager is a leader who is self-confident and respected, is responsible, holds themselves and others accountable, possesses personal power and can get others to work efficiently toward shared goals. Those who work with the Encourager do well because they are empowered made to feel worthwhile and important, and believe that they are an integral part of the achievement of the group's goals.

The Encourager instills commitment, rewards competence and maintains consistency. As a result, the Encourager develops a culture in which all can receive recognition and satisfaction in their work.

Those who work with an Encourager have admiration for the leader. Those who work above an Encourager put their confidence in the Encourager's ability to get the most out people, to get the job done. The Encourager sees crisis as an opportunity for enrichment and growth and will not mind making personal sacrifices. Encouragers see change as inevitable. This leader plans and utilizes resources to ease the transition from one task or goal to another.

The Stabilizer

This leader, by some means or another, is able to get the work done. The Stabilizer has the respect of some and the contempt of others. They typically have limited self-confidence and they take accountability only for that which the organization specifically requires.

People who work for the Stabilizer produce only the minimum required to get by. This type of individual hides their lack of personal power behind the mask of authority, which is used frequently. Those who work under the Stabilizer tend to "toe the line" while those who are peers tend to avoid this leader. The Stabilizer maintains a neutral work environment and brings to the organization only what he or she is paid to do, nothing more and nothing less. Stabilizers see crisis as a reflection of their management style; making excuses and finding reasons for not attempting to find answers outside of the comfort zone. Stabilizers seek to maintain the status quo and are passively resistant to change.

The Discourager

This leader lacks personal power, self-respect and the respect of others. Being somewhat irresponsible, a Discourager tends to blame rather than takes accountability and totally relies on authority and threats to intimidate subordinates to reach organizational goals. They have a "My way or the highway" mentality.

They typically are a "yes person" to those to whom they report. The Discourager creates an environment where very few can have their needs met. Their behavior restrains creativity, loyalty and hinders the innovation process. The Discourager uses crisis as a means to assert and increase his level of perceived power; using coercion and bullying as principle means of getting the agenda accomplished. Discouragers see change as a threat to their empire and work to undermine the positive effects of any modification; unless the modification is their idea.

"Encourage" good leadership

Throughout our development, we all may exhibit characteristics that are similar to each type of leadership, at one time or another. The goal is to understand what good leadership is and strive to emulate the role of the Encourager throughout our maturation process. It is helpful to identify Encouragers in your community to study and serve as examples to aid in your advancement. Once you have identified Encouragers, observe them, strike up a conversation, and start to incorporate some of their mannerisms and techniques into your character.

QUESTIONNAIRE

Answer the following questions:

1) Are leaders born or developed? Why?

_____

_____

_____

2) What are the 3 styles of leadership?

_____

_____

_____

3) What is your current leadership style? How can you improve?

_____

_____

_____

4) Which style of leadership should you adopt? Why?

_____

_____

_____

GAME ON: Tools and Strategies for Living on Purpose

Section 2: Defining Success

What is Success?

_____
_____
_____

How do you look when you are successful?

_____
_____
_____

According to the *American Heritage Dictionary*, "success" is a noun that means:

1. The achievement of something desired, planned, or attempted.
2a. The gaining of fame or prosperity.
2b. The extent of such gain.
3. One that is successful.

Most of us would probably agree with the first definition. After all, how can you know you have achieved success if you have not worked toward a desire, followed a plan or tried to reach a target, goal, or objective? Consider a trip to the mall. Most of us would say that our trip to the mall was a success if we were able to purchase the *perfect* outfit. Here "perfect" implies that the outfit met a set of criteria (price, size, or color) and finding the perfect outfit completed our objective.

So if we have not achieved something desired, planned or attempted, can we still be successful? Let's look at definitions 2a and 2b above. In view of that, "success" is the gaining of fame or prosperity and the extent of that gain. According to Andy Warhol, American pop artist, "we all get our fifteen minutes of fame," but let's focus on "prosperity" and "the extent of" that prosperity, which must be some kind of favorable gain.

We know we prosper when we reach a target, goal, or objective. But do we prosper on our way to reaching them? The answer most likely depends on your perspective of what "success" is. If you look at success as an end result, you will not see prosperity until you achieve your targets, goals and objectives. However, if you see success as a journey instead of a destination, you can see prosperity or favorable gain, with each step you take. Picture a ladder that you have to climb. Depending on the height of the ladder, your physical strength, aptitude and experience, climbing the ladder could be a struggle. But, each rung is a step that takes you closer to your goal of reaching the top. With each step you take you *prosper*. But what if you make a mistake, fall down a rung or are forced to take a step back? Are you still successful?

You can still consider a setback as a step toward a goal. Setbacks can actually propel you forward to reaching your goal. In fact, "setbacks" can even be more crucial to your success than "smooth sailing." Why? Because you learn more about yourself, your target, and the relationship between you and your goal each time you are required to take a corrective action. Think about it in terms of the ladder analogy, if your foot or hand slips while you are climbing, if you do not panic, you have the chance of shifting your weight to reposition your hands and feet to provide more stability and increase the chances of climbing the ladder successfully. In life when a setback occurs you have the option to reposition yourself for a better outcome.

On the other hand, you might determine along the way, through setbacks and implementing the associated corrective actions, that a particular goal is not right for you. This would be a successful realization even if you end up not achieving the goal. Time spent on goals that are not right for you or on goals you don't agree with or desire is wasted time. Why? In the process of working on goals that are not suited for you, you may lose out on an opportunity to do something else. Realizing this early, you can focus on the next dream, task, and next accomplishment.

You can pretty much find success wherever you look for it. The key is to look past your struggle, look at the big picture and never give up on yourself. As long as you are taking steps toward a goal, even small ones, then you are extending your prosperity in terms of a favorable gain. When you are taking steps to improve, regardless of size, you are as defined above, "one that is successful."

The following are quotes from "successful" people. Some of the people you may recognize and some you may not. The goal is to show that everyone's personal views on success are different. However, the one thing that most successful people have in common is the ability to overcome obstacles with determination and tenacity. Take a moment and read each quote and decide whether you agree with what the speaker is conveying from their experience.

Quotes on Success

"If you're trying to achieve, there will be roadblocks. I've had them; everybody has had them. But obstacles don't have to stop you. If you run into a wall, don't turn around and give up. Figure out how to climb it, go through it, or work around it."
-Michael Jordan

"The person who gets the farthest is generally the one who is willing to do and dare. The sure-thing boat never gets far from shore."
–Dale Carnegie

"Most successful men [women] have not achieved their distinction by having some new talent or opportunity presented to them. They have developed the opportunity that was at hand."
– Bruce Barton

"Would you like me to give you a formula for success? It's quite simple, really. Double your rate of failure. You are thinking of failure as the enemy of success. But it isn't at all. You can be discouraged by failure or you can learn from it. So go ahead and make mistakes. Make all you can. Because remember that's where you will find success."
– Thomas J. Watson

"Pity the man [woman] who inherits a million and isn't a

millionaire. Here's what would be pitiful, if your income grew and you didn't.
– Jim Rohn

"The great successful men [women] of the world have used their imagination... they think ahead and create their mental picture in all its details, filling in here, adding a little there, altering this a bit and that a bit, but steadily building - steadily building."
– Robert Collier

"The difference between a successful person and others is not a lack of strength, not a lack of knowledge, but rather in a lack of will."
– Vincent T. Lombardi

"Success is a journey, not a destination."
– Ben Sweetland

"No one ever attains very eminent success by simply doing what is required of him; it is the amount and excellence of what is over and above the required that determines the greatness of ultimate distinction."
– Charles Kendall Adams

The most practical, beautiful, workable philosophy in the world won't work - if you won't.
— Zig Ziglar

Notice, none of the quotes mentioned anything about success being based on luck, talent or family background. Each of the speakers focused their attention on things they can control like attitude, imagination, determination, preparation and taking advantage of opportunities. Success, then, is personal and depends solely on your ability to tap into your hidden potential. Remember, your path to success is unique because your definition of success is unique. Be careful not to define your personal success based upon someone else's standards or expectations. Why? Living in someone else's shadow can make you blind. It reduces you to stumbling through life one disappointment after another while attempting to find your own way. Ultimately, trying to live up to someone else's standards can be self-defeating and discouraging, causing self-doubt or negatively affecting your self-worth. This practice may be especially damaging if you do not buy in to the expectation and agree to take ownership of it. So, be free to be you. Set your own positive goals, take steps to achieve them and celebrate your accomplishments.

Becoming a Success

Remember, regardless of your personal definition, success is a possibility for you. The biggest barriers to success may often be failing to plan properly or the development of a negative self-image. Know that you are able to overcome both barriers. Let us look at a few tips for successful planning and how to better your self-image which will go a long way toward helping you to succeed (Hill, 1990).

Mistakes versus Success Secrets

Mistake 1: Using multiple tools and formats to collect your personal goals for success.
Mistake 2: Choosing goals that are unrealistic or not achievable.

Mistake 3: Writing out your goal, plan, task or project as one big singular clump.

Below are solutions to turning each of these unsuccessful practices into positive or successful outcomes. Following these *best practices* will turn your written words into effective actions.

Success Secret 1:

Create a goal or desire book to write down your thoughts. When you create a goal or desire book make sure it is in a bound notebook or a notebook with pages that will not easily fall out. It is often very easy, especially for a procrastinator, to start writing goals down then come back to it later. Eliminating the clutter will help you to focus on the task at hand and see it through to completion.

Success Secret 2:

It doesn't matter if you are writing down your goals or just thinking about them. Choosing goals that are unrealistic or not achievable is the best way to guarantee failure. For example, you can write down the goal of losing 50 pounds in one month but the bottom line is, this goal is NOT a realistic or in some instances an achievable goal. Make sure your goals are attainable, achievable and realistic. Then write them down!

Success Secret 3:

Clumping your goals, your plans, your projects or your tasks as one big singular sensation is one of the biggest mistakes anyone could make. It doesn't matter what the task is at hand. If you break your goals into smaller, easily achievable tasks, you will be better suited to prioritize those tasks and take the necessary actions through completion. As you write down your goals, use mind mapping techniques to help you break your goals down into actionable tasks. Working consistently on action-oriented tasks will result in success.

Self-Image

Developing a positive self-image is just as important as having and documenting a plan. In this section, we will discuss what self-image is and how to adjust a negative self-image if warranted.

What is Self-Image? Self-image is simply how you perceive yourself. It is a number of self-impressions that you have collected over time as a result of your life experiences. Self-Image is reflected by your answers to the following questions: What are your hopes and dreams? What is your reading of the world and why? What have you done thus far in your life and what do you long to do? What makes you happy? What brings you joy? One's self-image can be very positive, giving a person confidence in their thoughts and actions or it can be negative, making a person doubtful of their capabilities and ideas.

Some believe that a person's self-image is defined by events that affect him or her (i.e. doing well or not in school, work or relationships). Others believe that a person's self-image can help shape those events. For example, the most confident athletes, including those like Dwight Howard, now of the NBA's Houston Rockets, admit to spending time meditating on a positive outcome. In order to meditate on winning, athletes must first have the self-confidence that they can win. They also submit that achieving the expectations they have set for themselves becomes easier to attain each time they focus on believing.

There is probably some truth to both schools of thought.

Failing at something can certainly cause bad feelings, just as better performance on a project can lead to feeling good. But it cannot be denied that your self-image has a very strong impact on your happiness and your viewing of the world around you. Your self-image affects how you interact with those around you (Kimbro, 1991).

What do you believe…..?

Take the Test

How positive is your self-image? Answer these true or false statements and find out.

____ 1. My glass is always half-empty, not half-full.

____ 2. I'm always apologizing for things.

____ 3. I'm always telling myself I "should" be doing this or that.

____ 4. I constantly criticize myself.

____ 5. What other people think about me dictates how I feel about myself.

____ 6. I am critical of my mistakes and relive them over and over.

____ 7. I always let the people who care about me down.

____ 8. I feel like I have the weight of the world on my shoulders.

____ 9. A partial failure is as bad as a complete failure.

____ 10. I bend over backwards to please others.

____ 11. I am not sure I have done a good job unless someone else points it out.

____ 12. It's hard for me to forgive and forget.

____ 13. I have to work harder than others for relationships and I am afraid that the relationships I have will fail.

____ 14. If I don't do as well as others, it means that I am not as good as them.

____ 15. If I can't do something well, there is no point in doing it at all.

Results:
Give yourself **1 point** for each question you answered with "true".
0 - 4: You have a generally positive way of thinking and should feel good about yourself. Keep it up!
5 - 8: You may be struggling with some negative emotions. Take time to review your good qualities.
9 or more: You can be very critical of yourself. Challenge yourself to change your way of thinking (*Take the test*, n.d.)

If you scored above 5, do not panic. All hope is not lost. The rest of this section is dedicated to equipping you with the tools to help rebuild your self-esteem. There are several ways to improve your self-image but we will focus on two. Both will require your help to accomplish. The first has been mentioned several times in this book thus far – record and review your accomplishments. The second is developing self-affirmations and using your inner voice to remember your good qualities otherwise known as *self-talk* (Chapman, 1997).

Relive Triumphs: Record and Review your Accomplishments

It is easy to believe that you can achieve if you build upon one victory after another. Consider the process of learning how to ride a bike. Like most, probably for you the first step was letting go of the tricycle or "big wheel" and acknowledging that it was time for a bike. Getting used to being higher off the ground was an accomplishment. Soon you were mastering the art of riding with training wheels, building your self-confidence with each triumph. You probably dreamed of the day when you could ride your bike like the other kids without training wheels. Finally, you built up the courage to ride without this additional support or a parent's hand in the small of your back. At the beginning of the process and every time you fell, perhaps you could not picture the day that you would ride and do it successfully. But with each step, each victory you built a foundation for future successes and your view of yourself riding without support began to change. Take a moment and write a list of the things that you have completed, that you are most proud of and make it a practice to refer to this list often.

Self-Talk: Remember Your Good Qualities!

Reminding yourself of your positive qualities is another way to improve and maintain a positive self-image.
Use the following list as a guide or write your own list. What are you good at? What qualities do you have that make you feel good about yourself? What are positive things people have said about you? You may want to copy this worksheet and circle or highlight the words that describe you.

Put this list someplace where you can see it and remind yourself regularly of all your good qualities.

I AM...

Adaptable	Dynamic	Kind
Adventurous	Easy-going	Likable
Affectionate	Efficient	Logical
Ambitious	Energetic	Lovable
Artistic	Enterprising	Mature
Assertive	Enthusiastic	Merry
Broad-minded	Fair	Modest
Capable	Faithful	Natural
Caring	Flexible	Neat
Charming	Friendly	Non-judgmental
Cheerful	Funny	Nurturing
Clear-headed	Generous	Open-minded
Clever	Gentle	Optimistic
Compassionate	Glad	Organized
Competent	Good-natured	Original
Confident	Happy	Outgoing
Conscientious	Helpful	Patient
Considerate	Honest	Peaceful
Courageous	Hopeful	Persevering
Creative	Idealistic	Persistent
Dependable	Imaginative	Pleasant

Determined	Independent	Polite
Devoted	Industrious	Positive
Practical	Responsible	Trustworthy
Precise	Sincere	Truthful
Progressive	Sociable	Tolerant
Punctual	Spontaneous	Trusting
Rational	Spunky	Understanding
Realistic	Stable	Unique
Reasonable	Strong	Versatile
Reflective	Tactful	Warm
Relaxed	Talented	Witty
Reliable	Tenacious	Zany
Resourceful	Thorough	

Worksheet: (Remember your good qualities, 2004)

Above all, remind yourself who you are.

Defining Success

Why not take a few minutes now to write a description of yourself and include some of the nice things people have said about you.

GAME ON: Tools and Strategies for Living on Purpose

Section 3: Preparing for Success

Life is a journey and like any journey, be it a trip to Paris or a trip to the store you want to be prepared.

When you plan a trip to Paris you have to plan when you will leave, choose the airline, consider the weather, and decide where you will stay when you arrive and what you will do while you are there. The more details you have in your plan the more excited you will become in anticipation of your trip. The more research you do upfront, such as finding out the busy times for the museums and the Eiffel Tower (to avoid the rush) the more time you may have elsewhere for leisure. Instead of standing in long lines, your research will have you spend that time in a Bistro or café and going to the Eiffel Tower after the crowds die down.

Likewise, you are likely to make a list for trips to a store. Lists are important for keeping you on track when you shop. They help with keeping you on a budget to prevent over spending. Lists help you to save time. Lists equal forethought and preparation.

What are you planning to do?

_____

_____

_____

_____

Do you openly talk about being successful? Do you think about what your future will be? If you merely talk about it, you are leaving your future to chance or luck.

The way to achieve success is to have an action plan like the Paris example above. An action plan requires you to identify goals in all areas important to you. However, it is important to note that whatever you set out to achieve you want to do with honor. Being successful does not mean you will throw your values and morals out the window. You want to reach your goals with integrity and virtue and most importantly within the confines of the law.

What are you willing to do to achieve success?

_____

_____

_____

What are your goals?

When you wrote down your goals and desires, did you consider more than just goals for school and your career? A successful lifestyle will have balance. It may include college, career, family, and physical and social attributes.

Consider these things:

- *What am I curious about?*
- *What types of things do I enjoy reading about?*
- *What do I truly like to do?*
- *What do I find important?*
- *How can I make my community a better place?*
- *How can I mentor others?*
- *What things do I do to stay healthy?*

- *Do I spend quality time with my family?*

By creating an action plan your dreams and desires can become reality. The more detailed your action plan the more excited you will become about accomplishing your goals. Action plans provide you with a process for achieving success. Just like the old adage - How do you eat an elephant?

The answer is - One bite at a time. The elephant is big, and the idea of eating an elephant is overwhelming. However, if you think of eating the elephant bite by bite, eventually you will eat the entire thing.

This is also true for your big goals. They can be terrifying and it is easy to become overwhelmed by them. The answer is to break large goals down into smaller goals. The smaller goals get you on your way. As you achieve each smaller goal you are that much closer to accomplishing your larger goal which leads to success. This approach is called a *ripple effect* meaning small steps lead to big results.

Keys to Setting Goals

- Goals must be S.M.A.R.T. (Specific, Measurable, Attainable, Realistic, and Timely)
- Your goals must be important to you
- You must be willing to change your outlook (how you view and think about the world around you) to achieve your goals

S.M.A.R.T. Goals

Specific – Be specific and positive when setting your goals. You may have a goal to save the money you earn throughout the year to buy a home, to learn a new language, to learn to cook or to read a book a month.

Picture yourself attaining each of your goals. If you took a picture of yourself just after reaching your dreams, what would it look like? Develop your goals with this image in mind. You may want to start by asking yourself some basic questions:

- What do I want to accomplish?
- Who else is involved?
- Which requirements will I have to reach?
- Where will I have to go?
- When would I like to complete each task?
- Why do I want to reach this goal?

While you have a picture of your goals in mind, think of the words describing your accomplishment as the frame. You must frame your pictures with specific and positive words. A goal framed with negativity will blur your picture. For example if you say, "I'm not going without reading this summer." It is not a positive statement and can't be visualized. "I will read a book a month this summer" is positive. You can picture a book and the month as a specific goal. Imagining yourself accomplishing the goals you have set is the best motivation. Having a mental picture of yourself doing what you want to do is called **visualization.**

Measurable – Your goals must be measurable. Reading a book a month is simple to measure. Other goals seem to be harder to measure like learning a new language or leading a healthier life. These things can be measured if you formulate a system for measurement. For example, if you are learning a new language and initially you do not know anything about it or the culture in which the language is spoken you may want to measure your progress by keeping track of the time you spend on learning related material.

Perhaps you spend an hour in class twice a week and two hours each of those days outside of class practicing your lessons. At the end of a 30 day period you can measure the progress of how well you are learning that language. Conceivably you will be able to speak comfortably about the culture and to speak basic *everyday* words at that time.

To check to see if your goal is measurable, ask yourself:

- How will I know when the goal is accomplished?
- How much _____ is necessary?
- How many _____ will I need?
- How long will I have to commit to doing ___?

Attainable – When you begin planning your goals you will be able to identify what you find important. You will prepare yourself by gaining any skills you may lack, researching the subject and gaining knowledge to make the goals attainable. At this moment you will begin your journey to achieving the goals you've set.

Realistic - Realistic does not mean average. In fact, you don't want to have your goals be merely realistic, you want them to be set to stretch your reality. You want to have a challenge that you can achieve but not easily achieve. You want your goals to be something that challenge you and keep you sharp.

A realistic goal for running a marathon calls for a solid plan. Preparing for a marathon consists of a training program that lasts a minimum of five or six months, with a gradual increase (every two weeks) in the distance ran and finally a decrease (1 to 3 weeks) in the distance ran for recovery. The decrease, commonly called the *taper*, should last a minimum of two weeks and a maximum of three.

Timely – Your goals must be grounded within a timeframe. Without scheduling and setting timeframes for your goals (both small and large) you may not feel a true need to see them through. Without a deadline there is no sense of urgency and without urgency your goals are left to be realized someday. If you look on any calendar, you will notice there is no someday; it never comes. However, when you attach your goals to a specific timeframe, you've set your unconscious mind into motion to begin working on your goals and that day will arrive.

Your Goals Must Be Important to You

Loving friends and relatives may promote certain jobs or sports for you to pursue. They may want you to do things they think will best suit you and would like to see you involved in. Your loved ones have the very best intentions for you and certainly want you to succeed, but they cannot achieve your goals for you, the hard work is up to you!

You may need support and ideas from your friends and family but ultimately you will have the final say. Friends and family might make suggestions, but you control your future goals. Your goals should consist of plans under your control. Ultimately, your goals cannot be dependent on other people's behavior, decisions or choices.

Be Willing to Change Your Outlook to Achieve Your Goals

When you are setting your goals and while you are achieving them, your outlook must be positive. For some, it is not very easy to have a positive outlook. However, behaviors can be modified or changed to produce a positive outlook. An outlook is how one perceives and thinks about the world around him.

One of the first steps to changing your outlook is to remove negative words and phrases from your thoughts and conversations. Negative words create barriers to reaching the targets you set for yourself. Instead of saying "I can't" replace it with a question like "How can I?" Challenging yourself will allow you to identify solutions that may not have been apparent at the start. Self-discovery changes "I can't" to "I can". Determination changes "I can" to "I will". Here are a few more examples:

Barrier Words	Personal Challenges	Positive Words
I am not ...	What do I need to learn?	I am ...
I never ...	What is stopping me?	I always ...
I won't ...	Why?	I will ...
I hate ...	How can I become better?	I have the capacity

Ridding your mind of negative perceptions seems difficult but practice makes perfect. If you continue to strive to have a positive attitude, over time it will become second nature.

You want to be known as a person with a positive attitude. Positive people are more comfortable to be around. They are more confident, lively and they exude success. Opportunities are more readily available to positive thinkers. Think about it, if you were a business owner, who are you more likely to hire? Are you more likely to hire a person with a negative disposition or a positive one? Your success evolves from your attitude. Remember, nothing "succeeds like success."

To be triumphant, you must spend time daily without fail reviewing your attitude, checking your feelings and working on your mindset. You have the ability to control how you perceive things and think about the world around you. A positive attitude is the key to realizing your dreams.

QUESTIONNAIRE

Answer the following questions:

1. How do you eat an elephant?

_____

_____

_____

2. What are S.M.A.R.T. goals?

_____

_____

_____

3. What is success to you?

_____

_____

_____

4. Are you willing to change your attitude to succeed?

_____

_____

_____

Section 4: Background Check

As you begin to think about your future goals and aspirations, you will sometimes realize that the answers are not always clear cut about the choices you'll make, like:

- Graduating from high school or getting your GED
- Attending college or a vocational school
- Profession or career to pursue

Many times our circumstances and what others think can give us the belief that our goals and dreams are unreachable or unattainable. Most of the choices we make and our view of the world have been influenced by family, friends and peers. Growing up you may have been told you act just like your dad or your mom, or another influential person. Therefore, you may compare yourself, or try to achieve their status. In the process, have you abandoned or not focused on your own potential, goals and aspirations. The struggle to measure up can be a road block - and a difficult hurdle to get over.

Influence from Family

Two sisters are gazing at the newborn baby boy lying in the hospital crib. "Isn't he beautiful? And not just because he's mine." "Yes he is sis, and not just because he's my nephew." The two of them laughed and continued to gaze. They had a typical sibling relationship that allowed them to tease one another without ruffling one another's feathers.

After what seemed to be hours of the two gazing at the baby, he finally stirred, which was an opening for them to rush in and pick him up. "Well sis, I love my newborn nephew, but have you noticed he has his father's ears?" "Yes that's ok. He's perfect and just like the wolf said, "the better to hear you with my dear." "And look at these fingers; they are so long and skinny." "They are perfect too; these are the fingers of a great pianist or cellist." "Where are you going to find a cello in this neighborhood?" the aunt asked. "If I can't find one in the hood, I will bring one to the hood. Just so you know, he is a born leader and nothing you say or anyone else says will stop him," said the mom. "You know you sound just like daddy. He always saw the glass as half full."

As they sat there holding the baby, they thought back to how their father always had a positive outlook on life and taught them to do the same, never allowing obstacles to stop them. He saw obstacles as opportunities to achieve. So that is how they saw them too!

How successful do you think this child will be?

_____
_____
_____
_____
_____
_____

How important is the child's support system in his development?

_____

_____

_____

_____

Throughout our lives we are influenced and taught by many. It can have an effect on the way we view problems and events in our lives. As you have probably guessed, families have the most influence on an individual's personal, social and career development, more than school, work and even peer influence (Prinstein & Dodge, 2005). The family can have both a positive and a negative influence on their lives. If you take a moment to think about your household sayings, you could no doubt add numerous expressions, repeated statements, and life lessons that you have retained over the years.

Extensive research shows that parents are more influential in their children's lives than anyone else, shaping their thoughts, feelings and behaviors. Yet parents are neither the only influences nor the only ones with responsibility for the outcome. Peers, other adults, genetics, the media and various other sources also play important roles. Ideally, all these influences can work together, with parents, to promote healthy development in young people.

Parenting Styles

Children are influenced by parenting styles. We will take a look at four parenting styles, see if you can locate your parents' or loved one's style for raising you.

Authoritarian	This is a restrictive, punitive style in which the parents exhort the child to follow their directions and to respect work and effort. The authoritarian parent places firm limits and controls on the child and allows little verbal exchange. Children of authoritarian parents are often anxious about social comparison, fail to initiate activity, and have poor communication skills.
Authoritative	This style encourages children to be independent but still places limits and controls on their actions. Extensive verbal give-and-take is allowed, and parents are warm and nurturing toward the child. Children of authoritative parents are socially competent, self-reliant, and socially responsible.
Neglectful	This is a style in which the parent is uninvolved in the child's life. This style of parenting leaves the child feeling that other aspects of the parents' lives are more important than they are. Children whose parents are neglectful are socially incompetent. They show poor self-control and do not handle independence well.
Indulgent	This is a style of parenting in which the parents are highly involved with their children but place few demands or controls on them. Indulgent parents let their children do what they want to do which frequently leads children to expect to get their own way.

	Children whose parents are indulgent rarely learn respect for others and have difficulty controlling their behavior.

(Benson & Haith, 2009) [Chart]

As you begin to understand how you have been conditioned, you can now develop a process that will help you to become the person you're capable of becoming. Make sure to create conditions that ensure positive reinforcement and opportunities for positive conditioning.

Influence from Friends
Positive Influence

The ability to build meaningful friendships and develop healthy peer relationships depends on your sense of yourself as your own person - your self-identity, self-esteem and self-reliance (*Difficult Troubled*, n.d.).

Positive peer pressure can mobilize your energy to work hard, motivate you for success and encourage you to conform to healthy behavior. Peers can and do act as positive role models. Peers can and do demonstrate positive social behaviors. Peers often listen to, accept and understand the frustrations, challenges and concerns associated with being younger.

Positive influences encourage you to get back on track and re-focus when you have missed the mark.

Think about your own friends. Do they encourage you in positive ways?

Negative Influence

The need for acceptance, approval and belonging is a key aspect of your teen years. Teens who feel isolated or rejected by their peers — or in their family — are more likely to engage in risky behaviors in order to fit in with a group. For example, your friends may encourage you to come with them to a party where some of the "in" crowd will be. You know that your parents said you were not allowed to go because you needed to complete a science project or finish a core. When this happens, peer pressure can impair your good judgment and allow for risk-taking behavior, drawing a teen away from the family and its positive influences and pointing them towards dangerous activities (*Difficult Troubled*, n.d.).

A powerful negative peer influence can motivate a teen to make choices and engage in behavior that their own values and "common sense" might otherwise reject. Some teens will risk being grounded, losing their parents' trust or even facing jail time, just to "fit in." They would gladly risk it all to feel like they have a group of friends they can identify with and be accepted by. Sometimes teens will change the way they dress, their speech, give up their values or create new ones, depending on the people they hang around with (*Difficult Troubled*, n.d.).

Conformity

The process, discussed above, in which an individual's attitudes, beliefs and behaviors are influenced by other people, is called conformity. This influence happens in both small groups and in society as a whole. It may be the result of subtle unconscious influences or direct and overt social pressure blasted in the media.

Deciding how much to conform, or which group's values to conform to, are some of the major stressors for teens. Trying to conform to group behaviors that go against your own beliefs, in order to be accepted, creates internal conflict. This behavior also causes external conflict with family members and friends who attempt to intervene if they see you making "bad" choices. Defining oneself as an individual and developing a consistently strong value system forces young people to confront issues of conformity and non-conformity daily. This is a major challenge when growing up (*Conformity*, 2006).

"Many studies of young people show that if a person's friends engage in a behavior - anything from cigarette smoking to drinking alcohol to shoplifting to sexual activity - an adolescent is highly likely to conform to his or her friends' behaviors and try these activities. The alternative is for the young person to seek different friends with values more in line with their own. Often, however, the desire to be part of a group and the fear of social isolation makes it more appealing to change behaviors than to seek better friends" (Conformity, 2006, para.1).

Food for Thought: Conforming to the group's idea of right and wrong robs you of your uniqueness. It destroys your self-esteem and places more value on what someone else thinks of you than what you think of yourself.

Two questions you can ask yourself to evaluate whether or not you are conforming for the best are:

- Am I making this choice because it is the right thing to do?
- Am I going along with others just to fit in and please them, even though I know it doesn't feel like it's right for me?

Choices

Throughout life you will have the opportunity to make

choices and believe it or not, each choice you make has the power to change your life. There are many great opportunities and experiences that you can have available to you just by making good choices.

Things that you can change and have control over are:

- Your friends
- What you decide to do in the future
- What you think and how you respond to choices you have made

Then there are **things you cannot change** – things that you do not have any power over:

- Your family
- Neighborhood you grew up in
- Things that happened or that you did in your past
- Some of the physical features you were born with
- The weather

As you mature, you will start making more choices for yourself. One of these choices will be to surround yourself with positive influences and leave the negative people behind. This can be a struggle, but if you are able to act on this one simple but tough choice, it will lead you in a much more positive and promising direction – towards success.

Look Inside Yourself

Many times you may look to others, like family members and friends, for advice or direction because they may have life experience, good advice or are more knowledgeable in some areas. However, all advice is not good advice. All help is not helpful. It is good to listen to others, but it is just as important to listen to yourself. When you get advice from others, see if it agrees with your values and your goals, then decide on the right thing to do - for you.

QUESTIONNAIRE

Answer the following question:

1. The strongest value that I hold is my belief that:

_____

_____

2. The family value that was most impressed upon me is:

_____

_____

3. The values I have learned from my family affect many of the decisions I make?

Yes ____ or No _____

Please explain

_____

_____

_____

4. The way I would like to be seen by others reflects my values?

Yes ____ or No _____

Please explain:

_____

_____

_____

Section 5: Positive Perspective

There's a saying that "we are creatures of habit." This is pretty much true. The majority of the things we do on a frequent basis are a result of habits that we have accumulated. Habits are simply tasks, thoughts, ideas and processes that have been repeated to the point that they become a part of our routine and character.

Everyday Habits

Think about what you did before going to school. You get out of bed, take a shower, get dressed, eat breakfast, head off to school and go to class. It's all a part of your daily routine.

Some daily habits are beneficial because they are set up to help you accomplish your goals. Each time a task is completed, you become accustomed to doing it and more efficient at it (Ziglar, 2006). Soon it becomes instinctual. Some examples of good habits include:

- Studying
- Exercising
- Healthy Eating
- Being on Time

Some habits may not be beneficial for you. These habits you will need to examine and change if you want the larger pay-off of success. For example, if you are in the habit of coming home from school every day watching television, talking on the phone and hanging outside, instead of doing your homework and your chores, you may want to change those habits. You realize that habits like these may get you into trouble, or get you grounded with privileges taken away. But, the major consequence is: wasting time and robbing yourself of the opportunity to do something "greater later." Some examples of bad habits can include but are not limited to:

- Negative attitude
- Being late constantly
- Unhealthy eating habits
- Skipping class, poor or no study habits
- Drugs and/or Alcohol

Why Do People Develop Bad Habits?

Most people don't just set out to develop bad habits. Most often, a habit is formed without you ever realizing it. For example, people who bite their nails or crack their knuckles don't set out to develop this habit. It just happens over time and then it can be hard to stop. Sometimes learning a habit is easier than breaking it, so be cautious of the bad habits you are developing now because you will carry them with you into the future.

Developing Good Habits

Being able to develop good habits is so important to accomplishing your personal goals. Become serious about developing good habits! [HINT: For example, instead of thinking why changing is going to be so difficult, think about how you can do it.] One way to change habits is to actively remove bad habits and replace them with good ones. Think positive. Tell yourself you can and you will develop good habits. You will notice that you will have a positive attitude during the process as well (Ziglar, 2006).

You can develop good habits the same way you develop any habit; doing something over and over again makes it become second nature. Scholars agree that if you can repeat the same task consistently for approximately 21 days it can become a habit.

Attitudes

Attitudes are habits of thought.

Our "attitude" is the way we react to circumstances and conditions, based on what we have learned through our own experience - as well as the beliefs, values and assumptions that we hold. Attitudes show up as your actions and behaviors.

Our behavior in a given situation depends mainly on our attitudes toward the people and events involved - and they are even a give-away on how we feel towards ourselves. Our attitudes are developed early in life, so it is unfortunate when there have been more negative attitudes developed than positive ones.

If you want to make sure you are successful, you must begin right now, today, developing more positive thoughts and attitudes.

Your Attitude Controls Your Perspective

Your attitude about a situation controls how you will see that situation. Your attitude causes you to conduct yourself in a certain way and the way you behave will then determine the outcome of that situation. Therefore, your attitude determines your outcome. There is a correlation between attitudes, behavior and results. Consider the following formula:

Attitude + Behavior = Results

A good example of the importance of attitude is the story about a teenage boy whose parents wanted him to join the summer baseball team. He had been on the team for four years and wanted to switch to football instead. His parents really wanted him to play baseball because he was not "built for football." He joined the baseball team because he wanted to please his parents. He convinced himself that baseball was just for the exercise. When the first game arrived, he chose not to participate in batting practice or to throw the ball around, like the rest of the team. He thought to himself, "I'm not here to win. I'm just here for the exercise." He even snuck off to the snack bar and ate his fill of pizza and pop while his teammates warmed up.

You know the outcome of his game stats don't you? Yes, he struck out every time he came up to bat. He was too slow and sluggish to play in the field. He and his dad both knew that he had the ability to play baseball and could have done better and helped the team. What was the problem? His attitude was the problem. His heart was not in and this showed up in his behavior. When the boy got home and talked to his dad, the father suggested that he change his attitude.

For the next game, the boy warmed-up with his teammates and his attitude was positive, which gave him a different outlook, which gave him different results. In fact, he was even able to score the winning run. As you can see in this example, if your attitude is negative, your behavior will reflect that attitude.

The Power of Your Attitude

In any situation, you have a **choice** as to what attitude to embrace. There is no set of circumstances that dictate how you must react. There is nothing about any event or circumstance that requires you to feel upset. You make the **choice** about your own perspective, attitude and behavior. If you are upset about the way things turn out, that is the way that you **chose** to feel. And because you now understand the power of **choice**, you will notice that it is better to **choose** to react positively and reap prosperity than to **choose** to respond negativity and guarantee failure.

Think about your attitudes. Are they positive or negative? How would you respond if a loved one said, "That child won't ever amount to anything"? Would you say to yourself, "They are right. I can't do anything right," and give up without trying. This thought is based on a negative attitude and the behavior would show a negative result.

Or will you say to yourself, "I can do anything. I can try and do my best and prove that person wrong." You can **choose** how to react. This second thought is based upon a positive attitude that showed positive outlook, a "yes I can" attitude and the positive behavior will follow.

The reality that you are free to of **choose** to have a positive attitude will help you view situations in an encouraging light.

Choosing to Change Your Attitude

Sure, it's easy to just say, "Change your attitude and you'll change your life", (Ziglar, 1987). But how do you make that change if you don't know what to do? After all, if changing one's attitude was *easy* why wouldn't more people do it? Especially if it means they could be happier, more joyful, and much more successful?

The truth is, it's also easy to make that change. Changing your attitude doesn't need to be difficult. All you need to do is build that muscle by *consistently* putting into practice a few simple techniques. Then you'll be on your way.

1. **Think like you want things to be**

    Think ahead to how you'd like things to be – not behind at what you cannot change. It's tough to be happy, joyful and successful if you focus on the past, continue to relive negative experiences and refuse to expect the best for fear of disappointment. Think about what makes you happy and how you look when you are successful. Then do it!

2. **Smile and laugh often**

    Research shows that smiling and laughing have both psychological (mind) and physiological (body) effects on a person. For example, smiling and laughing trick the body into helping changing your mood. How? Smiling and laughter release chemicals into the nervous system that are linked to making us feel good. So, put a smile on your face and you'll be on your way to a change in attitude!

3. **Immerse yourself – Dive into new knowledge**

    Read books, articles and magazines that help you understand and adopt a new attitude. Watch films or listen to music that inspires you and encourages you to change.

4. **Change your actions**

    It's hard to change your attitude if you continue to rely on the same routine. Do things differently to start thinking differently.

5. **Change your environment**

    Make your environment reflect the attitude you wish to have. Create the physical space that makes you eager to change. Want to study better? Organize a study area!

6. **Follow the leader**

    Find someone who already has the attitude you wish to have. Follow their lead, learn from their example.

7. **Help others - and help yourself**

    One of the fastest ways to change your attitude is to take the focus off of yourself and to focus on helping others who are in need.

8. **Get a little help from your friends**

    Let everyone know you are looking to change. Enlist their help and get their ideas. The more you feel like you're part of a group effort; the more likely you are to be successful.

9. **Get a pro**

    If the change you desire to make is a big one or is extremely radical, consider getting the help of a mentor, counselor or coach. These people can help reduce the time and frustration involved in changing. They can provide new ideas to help you grow.

10. **Be patient**

    Recognize that most change occurs slowly, over an extended period of time. If you don't get immediate results, don't be surprised and DON'T QUIT! Keep working, it will come.

Your attitude creates your reality

To achieve success in your life and to become the leader you were meant to be, you must first see yourself as a winner. You must also see that same potential in others.

There's a story about a young man named Jim who was a customer service associate at a local fast food chain. His daily routine called for him to address and deal with many different attitudes from customers as he received and filled their orders.

One particular day Jim was challenged by a disgruntled customer who claimed that Jim deliberately filled his order incorrectly. Jim, using his effective communication skills, answered the gentleman's questions and corrected the order with such care that the customer left with a smile and a positive attitude. Jim also had an energetic customer who had no idea what he wanted to eat. Even though he spent more time than he wanted to on this transaction, overall it was a pleasant experience.

Jim's outlook and attitude toward his job and his customers allowed him to reach one of his potential goals. Currently, Jim works as a Shift Manager. When asked what he owed his success to, he replied, "Positive attitudes are contagious. I believe in keeping a positive attitude."

Many of us think our lives would improve if we could change other people. Not true, you have the power to change your attitude and influence others.

QUESTIONNAIRE

Answer the following questions:

1. What influence does an individual's family have on them and why?

_____

_____

_____

2. What is the difference between a positive and negative influence?

_____

_____

_____

3. How can conformity affect your decision making process?

_____

_____

_____

4. Why is it important to listen to yourself and follow your own mind?

_____

_____

_____

Section 6: Triumph Realized

Throughout this book we discuss success and what it means to different people. One person can have many definitions and measurements for how they perceive success. Success for education is measured differently than success with weight loss or writing a novel.

Earlier we illustrated the importance of goal-setting for success. Needless to say, that is not all you must do. The title of this chapter is Triumph Realized. Triumph is synonymous with success and it can't be realized without putting your goals into motion.

Planning a trip is not the same as actually taking a trip. A trip-plan for St. Thomas in the U.S. Virgin Islands, no matter how detailed, is not the same as being in that lush tropical paradise. It's nothing like actually sinking your feet into the warm sand on a beach along the ocean. It's nothing like smelling the ocean as you lounge on a hammock and listen to the water gently splash, crash and roar. It's nothing like enjoying the 80+ degree weather and 83 degree water of the Atlantic. And it's nothing like enjoying the fresh seafood caught only hours before it's prepared and delivered to your plate. In order to experience luxuries that this island oasis has to offer, at some point you must get on a plane or take a cruise.

All plans, whether they are for trips, weight loss, skill

development or life-long goals must at some point be put into action! If there is no action behind the plans, you are merely daydreaming. Plans are only as good as the execution.

Start recording your dreams, in all aspects of your life, develop and implement plans for reaching them.

Self-Assessment

Once you have made a habit of recording your dreams and developing action plans, start thinking about what it is going to take to reach those goals. Consider an Olympic sprinter. No race is ever decided at the starting blocks. Months of preparation have been put in before each race but at the starting blocks, runners still have to stretch, check the condition of their muscles, and assess their fitness level before the start. If they miss this step, it could cause an injury or a loss.

Perform a self-assessment to identify the resources you have and the resources you will need. Start asking yourself questions like:

What are my strengths?

- What skills do I have?
- What skills do I lack?
- How will I develop those skills?
- Will those skills help you in more than one aspect of my life?

What would you do if you could do anything you wanted? What goes on your "Love-To-Do List"?

- Would you like to "ace" every test you take?

- Would you like to earn an advance degree? Doctor? Lawyer?
- Would you like to travel to every continent?

The list is not for sharing with others, so be honest in your self-assessment and Love-To-Do-List. Consider this as a journey. When you go on trips to new places you want to seek out fun and exciting places. You want to try the best restaurants, shopping centers and visit the museums. When you explore yourself, be as thorough and visit just as many "places" in your mind. Write down your passions, your likes and your dislikes. Where would you like to make improvements in your life? What would you really like to do?

Establish Priorities

Most of us would agree that stepping into the starting blocks and running, without stretching and warming-up, would be silly and would risk injury. That's because you have to perform tasks in their proper order.

So, the next step after you complete the self-assessment is to prioritize your goals. There is a system to prioritization. You don't necessarily want to prioritize the easiest tasks first nor do you have to prioritize the hardest tasks first. The logical way to prioritize your goals would be according to the steps that need be taken to accomplish what must be done. Here is an example of prioritization. Some steps can be done without worrying about the other steps. Some steps require that other steps are completed first. In order to prioritize, you should start by asking, how tasks are related, and what are the consequences of performing tasks out of order. Consider the following example:

Cleaning Your Room

There are clothes all over, on the floor, on the bed, on the desk and on the chair. There is trash on the floor near the waste basket. Video games are out of their cases. Remotes are under the bed. Empty food containers are on the floor, dishes are under the bed. The bed is not made and the sheets have food stains from weeks ago. Where do you begin? Just like other goals, you must start at a logical point. You will prioritize your tasks in logical order. You won't begin with making your bed, so where will you start?

- Remove the dishes and food containers. Take the food containers and dishes to the kitchen.
- Pick-up and sort the clothes. Separate the clothes – clean or dirty.
- Hang the clean clothes or store them in drawers.
- Place dirty clothes in hamper or in laundry bag for dry-cleaning
- Place video games in their cases and store them properly.
- Place remotes in proper places.
- Place all trash in waste basket and empty waste basket.
- Remove dirty sheets and comforter (put in hamper).
- Put clean sheets and comforter on bed.
- Vacuum floor and dust furniture

Ta Da!! Your room is now clean! In this example, we can all agree that it would have been foolish to attempt to sweep the floor with clothes on it.

Every Problem Has a Solution

The solution to a problem may not always be apparent, at first. It could be a situation where you do not know what to do or what steps to take. It could be a barrier that is preventing you from moving forward.

As you accomplish your tasks and goals, you are certain to encounter problems or barriers that may threaten to slow your progress. Problems come in all shapes, sizes and arrangements. Problems could be circumstance-driven or people-driven. You won't always know how to solve your problems but you have to find a way. Do not shy away from the goal when you encounter difficulties, develop a system for identifying the solutions to the problems that threaten to slow you down.

Here is a systematic way to solving problems:
1. **Focus on the solved state**. The solved state is the goal. The problem is just a task that you must deal with on your way to triumph.
2. **Clearly define the problem**. Give an accurate description of the issue that you are facing. Be sure to include what the problem is, who it involves and the effect the problem has on you reaching your goals.
3. **Identify Probable Causes.** Think about all of the things that could be causing the issue. Be sure to include every possible cause – including unlikely causes.
4. **Identify the root causes.** Investigate and systematically eliminate causes that do not make sense. Then, focus on the causes of the problem that make the most sense.
5. **Identify Probable Solutions.** Determine solutions to the cause of the problem that you have identified. This can be accomplished in the following ways.

a. **Brainstorm.** Come up with ideas for how you may solve the problem and in the end you will decide on the most appropriate.
   b. **Research.** There may be known solutions to your problem. Read about them to see what works for you.
   a. **Consult others.** Don't hesitate to ask your family, friends and mentors to assist you with resolving issues.

6. **Take Action.** A problem cannot be solved if you don't take action to resolve the issue.
7. **Review and Assess!!!**

Here is an example to help illustrate how **systematic problem-solving** can be effective:

Tracey was a star on her school's varsity basketball team. She averaged 20 points a game and had the potential to be a college athlete. Her only flaw was that she could not be counted on to make her free throws consistently, even if the game depended on it. In her last 25 attempts, Tracey made only 12 shots. Frustrated with her performance at the free-throw line, Tracey decided to search for answers.

She started by focusing on the goal of making her free throws. Next she turned her attention to identifying her real problem with making these shots. Most of her shots were hitting the front of the rim or hitting the heel of the iron rim. Tracey looked at probable causes for her poor performance. She asked her coach about her technique. She also noticed that she had issues concentrating. She even convinced herself that her eye sight was starting to diminish, but an eye test confirmed that her eye sight was fine.

Triumph Realized

After discussing the issue with her father, her friends, and her coach, Tracey decided to focus on her power of concentration. She chose concentration because there were no obvious flaws in her technique. She spent several hours a day practicing her concentration techniques. She even paid her friends to attempt to distract her while she was shooting foul shots in the park. At the conclusion of each practice, Tracey would reflect on how well she concentrated and how that affected the way she shot the ball. She would then make changes accordingly.

Tracey saw her free throw percentage steadily increase from less than 50% to an average of more than 75%. Now Tracey is a prominent student athlete at a prestigious university. She owes her scholarship to her commitment to focus on and harness the power of concentration.

What can systematic problem solving help you accomplish?

_____
_____
_____
_____

GAME ON: Tools and Strategies for Living on Purpose

QUESTIONNAIRE

Answer the following questions:

1. What is triumph? What is a "win"?

   _____

   _____

2. What is necessary for achieving success?

   _____

   _____

3. What do you accomplish when you assess yourself?

   _____

   _____

4. Why is it important to establish priorities?

   _____

   _____

5. What are the critical steps in solving a problem?

   _____

   _____

Section 7: Action Planning

Lights! Camera! Action!

You now have more insight and understanding about yourself and what you want out of life. You have put your desires into words and have a plan to succeed. What's next? **ACTION!** You must now put your plan into action. You must follow through with your plans to accomplish your goals.

PROCEED WITH CAUTION!!!

As you prepare to take action towards accomplishing your goals you want to be aware of some roadblocks so that you may avoid them.

Frustration

Even though your goals excite you and you are determined to accomplish them, there may be an occasion for frustration. Important goals can seem overwhelming which, in turn, may frustrate you.

Do not be alarmed, feeling overwhelmed is normal. There are things you can do to alleviate the frustration so that you may continue pursuing your goals.

- Re-evaluate your plan. Make sure your goals are realistic and the time tables are not too short.
- Make sure you are not procrastinating. When you delay your tasks, you may feel an enormous amount of stress as you play catch-up.

- Don't be afraid to make mistakes. Remember mistakes can be great teachers.
- Remember the old adage, "if at first you don't succeed try, try again."
- Check your confidence level. If you find yourself asking "Can I do this?" Say emphatically, "YES I CAN!"
- Don't be afraid to enlist help from others when evaluating where the frustration may be coming from.

Fear

Fear is a natural emotion that is driven by the expectation or recognition of exposure to negative consequences in the form of harm, pain or loss. Scholars agree that fear can take many forms. Some fears are founded and rooted in reality, based on fact or on a series of experiences, while most are developed out of a feeling of insecurity. For example, you could be afraid of falling from a ten-story building. It is true that a fall from that height would definitely harm you, especially if you are working on a roof without the proper safety equipment. Your experience from falling from lesser heights would be enough to prove to you that harm would occur. However, if you still believe you are going to fall looking out of a fixed panel window of a ten-story building, you would lack the faith in the security of the window to keep you from falling. Most of us would agree, in the latter example, that the chances of you falling through the glass are unlikely. In this case, you would be guilty of developing an irrational belief about how looking out of the window will result in a disastrous or unsettling penalty for you. It would be an unsound concern that only existed in your imagination.

The degree by which we feel fearful is relative to our sense of vulnerability. The effects of being vulnerable can be debilitating, cause stagnation and prevent us from living a productive and prosperous life. Fear can be the underlying motive behind inaction and the behaviors that block clear thinking, problem solving and decision making abilities. The unwillingness or inability to think or move is the result of irrationally surrendering power and control of your thoughts to an object, person or circumstance. For example, fear of test taking may cause you to freeze or not answer the questions properly.

The most common fears are learned and can be traced back to our families, our environments, our habits we develop, and our experiences as we mature. If your parents were afraid of "being broke" and took extraordinary steps to save, odds are they instilled that fear in you. You will find yourself stockpiling mason jars and other containers to store pennies and coins, hoarding food, and keeping clothing that you may have out grown. Likewise, if you grew up in a rough neighborhood, you may fear the possibility of getting robbed at a bus stop. You may find yourself being overly cautious in the type of clothing, shoes, and jewelry you choose to wear in your neighborhood. Often you may avoid the bus all together.

Often, fear can be used as a crutch. Those who are fearful of change, use fear to support their unwillingness to alter or modify "comfortable habits." They often make excuses to mask weakness and avoid growth. For example, a student may use the risk of failing to continue cheating. People who fall into this category are usually opposed to asking for or accepting offers of help from others. They are worried about being thought of as weak or are concerned that the individual offering the help will think less of them.

Do you know anyone like this?

Research has also shown that some of the things that we are fearful of change over time while some are ingrained in our personality. A child who is afraid of the dark may become a teen who is afraid to fail. Conversely, a child who is afraid of being alone may become an adult who has the same aversion to loneliness.

Not all fear is bad. Fear can also have a self-preserving and motivational quality pushing you to reach beyond your comfort zone to be successful. This "good fear" compels us to better ourselves and fosters enrichment and personal growth. For example, the fear of losing forces us to find ways to win. The fear of failing causes some to invent new strategies to improve study habits. The fear of being left behind may foster perseverance.

Common Fears

In this stage of your development, most people would be afraid of failure, rejection, the unknown, what other people may think about you and disappointment. We will spend the majority of this section discussing each fear.

Fear of Failure

The fear of failure may stop you from reaching your goals. The idea of failure may cause some to resort to cutting corners, cheating or even giving up trying. Cutting corners, cheating and giving up each have associated consequences and may also lead to failure. In the case of cutting corners, valuable steps or pieces of information could be missed in the search for instant gratification. As a result, the project may not meet the specified goal and cause personal regret. In terms of cheating, regardless of skill level, offenders will eventually get caught. Most cheaters become over-confident, begin to underestimate risk, and start to make mistakes which lead to failure. Finally, not trying or giving up, negatively affects your level of confidence. Seeing someone else try and succeed may only lead to regret.

The truth is, we all make mistakes and from time to time those mistakes will result in failure. The difference between truly successful people and those who wish for success is the way they see failure. Truly successful people see failure as an opportunity to learn and grow (Maxwell, 2009). Typically, they welcome failure because it provides useful information on how they can improve. Most of the richest people in America have made and lost fortunes several times. Each time they fail, they assess and think about where they went wrong. They develop strategies and corrective actions to address the problems that lead to failure. They implement solutions and seldom make the same mistakes again. There are lessons to be learned from failure. Learn the lessons and turn your failure into success.

Fear of Rejection

The fear of rejection can stop us from asking questions, making new friends or even pursuing a new love interest. The thought of a person telling you "no" or "they are not interested" in what you have to say or what you think can be devastating. The effect on your self-esteem can be painful.

The need to be accepted is a powerful need. But the reality is that everyone is not going to like or accept you. Rejection is a part of life. Some people are not secure enough or happy with whom they are and build their self-worth at the expense of someone else. Do not take it personal, it is more a reflection of their insecurity and not your own. However, if you play into it, you relinquish your control, making you less secure and vulnerable to fear. Do not allow rejection to hurt your self-esteem. Be true to yourself. You are capable of great things. You are strong and you have some attributes that are appealing to friends and loved-ones. Find out what they are and capitalize on them. Don't allow criticism from others to come between you and success. You are the only person that can hold you back.

Fear of the Unknown

Not knowing what is going to happen can be frightening. The future is not known to anyone. Anything can happen. You could lose a loved one. The country could go to war. Your parents could lose their jobs. What is worse homelessness can become a concern. Any of these things would be traumatic and life changing. You can recover from them all and still be successful. You could spend time dreaming up a lot of negative outcomes or you can dream positive ones. You could continue to come up with excuses not to try or you can strive to achieve. You could continue to waste time or make good choices with the time you have been given. You can control how prepared you are for the future.

You cannot control the weather, the stock market, or the economy but you can plan and strategize for them based on available information. If your plan is to go to college, you can prepare by studying and maintaining good grades. You can excel on the pre-college entry exams and narrow your educational choices by talking to counselors. You can arrange financing by applying for scholarships. Plan, implement and control the things you can control and tomorrow will take care of itself.

Fear of what people will think

Like most fears, the fear of what others may think will cause a variety of behaviors. This fear could manifest itself in inaction, doing something really "stupid" or failing to do the right thing. Fearing what people think can completely change your identity and can cause you to succumb to peer pressure. Living your life wondering what other people will think will stunt your growth and place your own big personality in a very small box. For example, if you fail to apply yourself in school because you think you will be thought of as a nerd, you are developing the habit of not being assertive. By not asserting yourself, you may open the door to a life full of mediocrity and regret. A teen who is not assertive becomes an adult who is not assertive. Adults who are not assertive develop dysfunctional relationships, are passed over for promotions or get taken advantage of in the work place; often times accepting too much responsibility because they will not say "no".

The key to being successful is applying the knowledge that you have, learning new skills and implementing planned strategies. Some of your thoughts and ideas will not be popular. Share them anyway. As we stated above, your loved ones and true friends will still care about and support you regardless of what you do or how "embarrassing" you may think you are. Speak up for yourself. Have the courage to be you and do the right thing.

Fear of Disappointment

The fear of disappointment will cause you to unjustly lower your own expectations. It will rob you of your incentive to try and your motivation to set goals for yourself and others. Like the fear of rejection, it can also stop you from developing meaningful relationships. You will avoid making or keeping friends because you will be concerned with them letting you down. You will also be less likely to ask for help because you will feel that "I am better off doing it myself."

The fact is, even the most trustworthy person you can think of will eventually let you down. Humans are human. We all make mistakes, even sometimes with the best intentions. Sometimes we even let ourselves down. Therefore, disappointment is a part of life. Be careful. Do not set unfair expectations for yourself or for others. Setting unfair expectations for yourself will negatively impact your self-esteem. Setting unfair expectations for others will destroy your perception of who they are and will cause conflict in the relationship.

One of the tricks to nullifying the effects of possible disappointment is to re-evaluate your expectations based on the capabilities of the people and circumstances involved. Next, understand that "things" happen that are outside of your control. Then, identify possible barriers to reaching your expectations. Finally, think of an alternative plan and be prepared if differing circumstances arise. For example, if you planning to attend a party make sure you have an alternative ride to and from the party in case your original plans fall through.

The other trick is to learn to "think on your feet." The ability to think quickly and make the necessary adjustments when things appear to be going wrong will greatly reduce the chances of a negative outcome and disappointment. Focused, confident improvisation greatly increases the possibility of getting the outcome you expect. If you are expecting to win a basketball game with time running out, you see that the prescribed plan is breaking down, so you cut to the basket, receive a pass and you score and win. Most would agree that you have done the right thing. But what would have happened if you did not improvise?

Suggestions for Coping with FEAR

➤ Remember everyone has fear. Fear is a learned response to the issues that we face. The best thing about learned behavior is that things can be "unlearned" and our behavior can be modified. The first step in coping with fear is to acknowledge that you are afraid. Most of us are too proud to admit even to ourselves that we are terrified of change or the unknown. In order to be successful, we must summon the courage to be honest, to identify the cause of our fear, change our attitude about it and confront it. We must take steps to get the power that we have surrendered to that thing, that person, that circumstance, back.

➤ Remember fears are thoughts. The extent that we feel afraid is relative to our own assessment of our self-confidence and our ability to effectively utilize the resources that we have at our disposal to deal with a perceived threat. From the preceding Sections, you learned that you are in complete control of your own self confidence and you are capable of wielding the tools in your toolbox to regain your personal power. Restore your confidence by reclaiming your thoughts. Remove the negative thoughts and emotions by thinking positively. Have faith in your abilities. Exchange feelings of fear for attitudes of faith. Focus on the positive advantages of health, satisfaction and achievement instead of the consequences of harm, pain and loss. Focus on your accomplishments. Remind yourself of your attributes.

Drown out negativity. Remember, you are resourceful.

➤ Turn fear into bravery. As you begin to confront your fear, it is only natural to have butterflies. Take comfort in your ability to stand. Be courageous and resilient. If you fall, get back up. You will notice that with every experience you will get stronger. You will find that the more you successfully handle fearful situations, the less vulnerable you will feel. The reward is more self-confidence and another victory by which you will be able to build additional victories. Soon, you will have overcome your fears and will be well on the path to being successful.

Action Planning

QUESTIONNAIRE

Answer the following questions:

1. How will you cope with fear?

_____

_____

_____

2. Can fear be positive?

_____

_____

_____

_____

3. How will you get help when you get frustrated?

_____

_____

_____

Section 8: Time Management

You can regain most of the things in life you have lost. The only commodity that cannot be replaced is **TIME**. Up to this point, the things we discussed are all things that you can regain control over – your attitude, your thoughts and your ability to plan and implement strategies for success. You can even work hard and replace material things. You can purchase gym shoes, cars, and jewelry to replace items that have vanished. But you cannot make more time. A minute that is wasted cannot be returned. With each passing day, you are getting older and you do not get a chance to relive yesterday. Therefore, you must take advantage of every opportunity to spend your time wisely.

Time Management is a tool that is designed to help keep us on target and it allows us to "make the most of our time." Time Management techniques are aimed at effectively managing work-loads, allocating resources and juggling tasks. Good Time Management improves productivity by helping us focus our efforts, assisting us in keeping track of errands, appointments and assignments. Failing to use good Time Management causes undue stress and frustration due to the extreme pressure caused by cramming, being "up against deadlines." To summarize, the purpose of using good Time Management techniques is to prevent us from wasting time on the road to success.

Common causes of wasting time:

Distractions

Distractions are anything that interrupts, replaces or prevents you from reaching your goal by the appointed deadline. Distractions can be internal or external. An example of an internal distraction can be unsettling emotions, when your mind races with concern over people or events. That's an energy drain.

External distractions can take many forms and can range from texting to television, iPods to idiots, or from pimples to people. Even a small well-intentioned side conversation, as simple as it is, can prevent you from reaching your goal for the day. To prevent succumbing to distractions, concentrate on the goal and take action to limit access to the object of distraction by practicing self-control.

Examples of distractions are:

- **Focusing on things that are outside of your control**

    Focusing on things that are outside of your control robs you of time that would be better spent on things that you can control. To spend a huge amount of time focusing on the past, on your background, or on what others think is a waste of your time. The only thing you can do about what has happened in the past is to learn from it. To repeat it over and over in your mind is a waste of time. You cannot change what has happened, but you can change what will happen. You can control yourself. You can control your thoughts, your attitudes and how well you work toward your plan for success.

➤ Poor Planning

Poor planning and forgetting to plan ahead lead to poor decision-making. Without a written plan, tasks and the steps needed to complete them are forgotten, omitted or completed out of sequence. Time is spent stopping, back tracking, reviewing and correcting these problems. In most cases, time could have been saved if a moment was taken to brainstorm; allowing each detail to be thought out and written down. Proper preparation prevents poor performance, disappointment and, in some cases, regret.

➤ Misplaced Energy

When time is wasted on completing tasks that are not related to the goal, this is misplaced energy. More time is needed to re-focus, get back on track or "play catch up." Some causes of misplaced energy can be:

- Failing to say no to outside tasks and accepting unnecessary responsibility
- Spinning because of big goals, biting off more than you can chew
- Failing to read or fully understand all that goes into the project or task
- Listening to and participating in useless conversations
- Allowing others to dump their emotional baggage on you

➤ Not setting and sticking to priorities

Failing to set priorities guarantees that some important items will be missed. Misplacing energy, you may spend more time on less important items, leaving little to no time to focus on larger more important ones.

HINT: Set short-term priorities. List all tasks then re-arrange tasks in order of importance. Refer to the list often and make changes as necessary. Be flexible. Situations and circumstances may arise that shift your priorities. Remember, in order to be successful you will have to develop and establish a system for setting priorities.

⭒ Cluttered Rooms and Work Spaces

Working in a cluttered work space can be time consuming. Time is wasted looking for papers that are hidden by unnecessary objects and debris. Time that is spent partially cleaning portions of your workspace is wasted time. In some cases, money is also wasted because items are repurchased before they are found. Keeping your room and work areas clean reduces the amount of time it takes to perform simple tasks. Consider how much time you would save if you didn't have to hunt for the outfit you wanted to wear, look for the toothpaste, play "where are my keys," or search for tools. Develop a system of organization.

⭒ Misplaced Information

You waste time when you can't find critical papers and documents, because you don't remember where you put them. Consider placing important documents, such as college applications, your license app and scholarship essays in a labeled folder or portfolio. Place them in a specific spot, like a file cabinet, as soon as you get them.

⭒ Waiting

Waiting is considered a waste of time. It is idle time

that could be used to do something else. But many times, waiting can't be avoided. To minimize the time you have to wait, always call and confirm your plans the day before. It is also a good practice to call the day of, just to make sure your appointment or other plans have not changed. In cases where waiting is unavoidable, like at the doctor's office, it is a good idea to arrive less than 30 minutes early and to carry something to work on. Even if the only thing you do is review and revise your schedule and Time Management plan, you are one step closer to reaching your goal when you make time work for you.

↳ Procrastination

When you put a task off until another time or day you can consider that procrastination. Procrastination is a destructive habit for anyone in leadership. Pushing your goals off until tomorrow can lead to lost opportunities. Working on your goals consistently will keep you moving in the right direction. Examine why you are procrastinating? Are your goals too big? Do the barriers to achievement seem too great to overcome? Remember, you have the power to shape your own destiny – your own TRIUMPS. Lofty goals can be broken down into attainable tasks and steps. Barriers and problems have solutions. The only thing left is to stop making excuses and stop wasting **TIME**!

Remember time is a precious commodity. Use time wisely. If you waste it, you will lose an opportunity to reach your full potential.

↳ Making the most of your time

Since time is a finite resource, the next step in ensuring the future you want is understanding how to **use time to leverage opportunities**. HINT: Tips to develop your own

GAME ON: Tools and Strategies for Living on Purpose

Time Management system. In order for this process to work, you must take ownership and use the techniques to create a system that works for you.

- **Take time to plan and schedule tasks.** Planning reduces the time associated to a given task by making sure that all the steps and resources are accounted for.

  - **Think on paper.** Write everything down and do not trust your memory. Make a list of everything that must be done, the deadline to complete the task, and you'll be closer to your target.

  - **Keep it simple.** Make your notes easy to read and understand. Feel free to use abbreviations. Do not worry about spelling and grammar. Remember, these are private notes and you are the only one who must understand the system.

  - **Be convenient.** Use your cellular phone to capture notes and dates in its calendar. If you do not have access to a cell phone, carry a small notebook with you. If you don't keep your plans near you, you will forget them and your plans will then be useless.

  - **Prioritize.** Consolidate similar tasks. Decide how you are going to prioritize tasks and organize them by writing down the order in which the task must be completed.
      - Think ahead. Identify all of the resources that will be needed to complete each task. Include the cost, risks and rewards of each task.

- **Be organized.** Verify that work spaces are clean and that all items, paperwork, documentation and tools are stored in a designated place. Make a habit of putting things back where they belong and you will know where they are when you need them.

- **Set deadlines.** Think about how long it will take to realistically complete each task and assign deadlines for each task. Take action immediately to ensure tasks are completed by the deadline.

- **Review.** Review your plans daily. Review your priorities often; change them according to their relative impact on your short term and long term goals. Remember, plans that are **out of sight** become **out of mind**. Place a copy in your locker, by your night stand and by the mirror in the bathroom, if necessary.

- **Learn to use idle time.** Time spent doing nothing can be better used doing something else. Use "down time" to catch up on making phone calls, to work on assignments, or to make plans. Also, plan well, to reduce idle time.

- **Learn to say "no."** Learn to say no to yourself as well as others. Say no to yourself by practicing self-control when you are tempted to take extended breaks, perform task out of order, or procrastinate. Say no to others when they attempt to add tasks to your schedule that you don't have time for or that don't align with your goals or values.

- **Learn to delegate tasks.** Think of tasks that you do that can be done just as well by someone else. Approach the person who can handle the task and ask if they can help you. Then transfer the task. HINT: For example, you are working on a group project and the group is falling behind because one of your tasks is taking longer than you expected. It would be in the best interests of the team, if you asked one of the other students to help with your task so that the team meets the deadline.

- **Reward yourself for completing tough or important tasks before the deadline.** Celebrate your accomplishments in Time Management. Recognizing your victories builds your self-esteem and gives you the confidence to develop a working plan, to push through distractions to overcome your personal struggles and meet deadlines.

- **Remember** - developing and practicing good Time Management techniques will keep your schedules drama-free, minimize the need for crisis management and reduce the stress associated with always having "your back against the wall."

Other Time Management Tips

In additions to developing a good system for planning and managing your time, you also will need to be flexible. Here are a few things to consider:

Balance your schedule. As you begin to organize and prioritize your studies, activities and job-related tasks, remember to schedule time to spend with friends, family and on things that you enjoy doing. Every schedule must have balance. Include time for fun, hanging out with friends, attending family gatherings or working on a personal hobby – or you will just ignore your schedule. A balanced lifestyle is needed to be efficient, successful and happy.

Be careful of double-booking. Reviewing your schedule and keeping it with you will reduce the likelihood of double-booking. But in spite of your best efforts, scheduling conflicts will occur. Remember, plans are not set in stone. You can always change the plans that only really affect you – the ones that you can control. You may not be able to reschedule your loved one's birthday party, friend's wedding, or your history test - but you can reschedule trips to the mall, time to play video games and breaks. Do not be afraid to postpone or reschedule. People prefer "notice" to a "no show."

Try not to plan so far in advance that things are bound to change. Attempting to plan too far in advance may become distracting and cause you to miss out on an opportunity, all based on plans that may not end up happening. Only plan for events that you feel are fairly certain to take place.

Be flexible and allow time for spontaneity. Remember everything does not always go according to plan. Events can occur that we have no plan for. For example, friends may come into town unexpectedly, a loved one may fall ill. You have to have some leeway to live or the schedule itself can cause stress. Allow time for changes and develop alternative plans as needed.

GAME ON: Tools and Strategies for Living on Purpose

Time Management Aids

➤ **Create a simple "To Do" list**

This program will help you identify: a) a few key tasks, b) the reason for doing them, c) a timeline for getting them done. You would then print this list and post it for reminders. Remember to prioritize.
- Make of the list of items that you must complete.
- Read through the list of tasks and assign a priority to each task by labeling the most important task with the first letter or number. (#1 –or- A)
- Re-arrange the tasks in order of priority and post it where you are likely to see it every day.
- Refer to the list often and make changes as necessary. Remember, be flexible. If situations and circumstances arise, push items back or pull items forward to compensate.
- The key is consistently working to complete the tasks on the list.

➤ **Daily/Weekly Planner**

Write down appointments, daily assignments, classes and meetings, on a calendar, log book or chart.
- Arrive earlier to appointments, classes and meetings
- Once a day, check what's ahead for the day
- Always go to sleep knowing you're prepared for tomorrow

* Remember the old adage: **"To be early is to be on time, to be on time is to be late and to be late is unacceptable."**

➤ Long Term Planner

Use a monthly chart or calendar so that you can plan ahead. Long term planners will also serve as a reminder to plan time for your goals.

By using the techniques that we have discussed in this section, you will be equipped to manage yourself and others, to make better use of your time. Plan and take advantage of every opportunity. **Success is yours for the taking.**

QUESTIONNAIRE

Answer the following questions:

1. What are some of the common ways that you waste time?

_____

_____

_____

2. What is procrastination?

_____

_____

_____

3. Is procrastination ever positive?

_____

_____

_____

Section 9: Effective Communication

Communication with others is the key to your success!

Communication is defined as: "A process by which information is transferred or exchanged between individuals through a common structure of speech, symbols, signs or behavior" (U.S. Congress, 1990, p.31). Communication is any expression of thought. It can be simple as conveying an idea through a familiar gesture, voicing the answer to a question or stating a purpose. Information can also be conveyed in art, poetry or song.

Communication is a multi-faceted process with a) the sender, b) the message, and c) the receiver. A message is conveyed by a sender to a receiver via a channel/medium. The receiver then decodes the message and gives the sender feedback. The process is **successful only when the receiver receives the message intended by the sender**. But, if the message is misinterpreted, that is miscommunication, the source of confusion.

It's written all over your face

There are three major elements to face to face communication: 1) body language, 2) voice tonality, 3) words. According to communication research:

- 55% of the message is interpreted based upon the

body language – the posture, gestures, and eye contact – of the sender.
- 38% of the message is interpreted based upon the tone of voice of the sender.
- 7% of the message is interpreted based upon the words used to convey the message.

Dialogue or Verbal Communication

A dialogue is a reciprocal (back and forth) conversation between two or more people.

<u>Non-verbal Communication</u>

Non-verbal communication is the process of communicating through sending and receiving wordless messages. The messages can be communicated through motion, body language, facial expressions and/or eye contact. On a daily basis, we consciously and unconsciously use non-verbal communication to send cues about our mood to those around us, at home, work and play.

Non-verbal communication is the most significant piece of communication. The majority of our emotions and the subtle nuances of our personality are telegraphed by our facial expressions. For example, if we do not agree with something a friend is saying without realizing it, there may be a frown on our face.

There are times you may intend to mask your true feelings with words you don't mean. But you must pay close attention to your body language or you may reveal your true thoughts or confuse the receiver of your message. Despite your best efforts you're your words, your body language will tell the true story. When you communicate with skilled readers of non-verbal cues, you may not be able to hide what you are feeling. Your voice and words may say one thing, but your body language including the tiniest facial expressions and movement can give you away.

Tips for Decoding Non-verbal Communication

- People communicate on many levels simultaneously. Watch their facial expressions, eye contact, posture, hand and feet movements, body movement and overall appearance. Every gesture is conveying something, if you listen with your eyes.
- If a person's words say one thing and their body language says another, listen to the body language - it usually tells the truth.
- "When leading a group, recognize that non-verbal cues can tell you:
  - when you've talked long enough
  - when someone else has something to say
  - the mood of the crowd and the effect you are having on them".

Pay attention to these things and you'll be a better leader and speaker. Just remember understanding non-verbal communication improves with practice.

Effective Communication

Communication is one thing, but effective communication is another idea altogether. Effective communication begins with:
- The ability to effectively translate a concept into another person's language
- The skill to break down information to a level that your audience can understand'
- The ability to persuade others to accept your point of view

- Active listening and observation

The foundation of effective communication is the notion that everyone is unique, has value and is able to contribute. This form of communication respects all points of view. It accepts, but not necessarily agrees, with what is said. It believes that everyone has the right to their own opinion and fosters understanding, consensus and resolution.

The effective communicator understands that most people abandon logic when emotionally charged, when angry or confused. Effective communicators do not seek to assign blame, only to resolve issues.

Effective communicators realize that conversations are interactive and require participation from all parties involved. If the other party is not engaged in the conversation, the effective communicator finds ways to peak their interest about the subject. Effective communicators must be willing to accept that people process information differently.

Active listening

Recognize the importance of listening and make it a key part in your communication style.

Show your readiness to listen by paying close attention to the thoughts and feelings of the other person. Showing interest by nodding or using occasional verbal responses such as "uh-huh" indicates you are "hearing" or "validating" the speaker.

- When listening, paraphrase what you've heard. Paraphrasing lets the other person know you are trying to understand.

- Ask open-ended questions when clarification is needed. Ask who, what, when, where and how.

- At the end of the conversation, summarize what you have heard. Make absolutely sure you understand the speaker's intent.

- Be cautious about giving an opinion or advice. Don't give it if the speaker declines.

Active listening shows and encourages empathy, compassion for or understanding of others. A good leader will have the quality of understanding the needs of others.

Put your active listening skills to the test. Be quick to listen and slow to speak. Leave the person feeling that they have gotten their point across. Force yourself to become an active listener. Learn to set aside prejudices and pre-conceived notions. Do not jump to solutions without fully understanding the problem. Remember, practice makes perfect.

Tips for Communicating Effectively

Here are some additional tips to become an effective communicator.

Know Your Audience

One of the first steps in learning how to communicate effectively is to know and understand your audience. Each person has a distinct communication style, a unique way of processing information and a limited capacity to relate. Effective communicators must be able to identify how the other person communicates and assigns value to what they hear.

Think about what is required to talk to a person who does not speak English. In spite of your best efforts, the person will not understand you because the non-English speaking person cannot place a "value" on your words. Likewise, if we use slang or phrases that the listener does not understand or deems to be inappropriate we can alienate our audience. The use of excessive or inappropriate jargon, slang, or buzz words could leave some of the listeners feeling unable to relate. As a result, the listener may disregard what you say – even if what you are trying to convey is profound. The key is to translate your concepts into words that the hearer can easily digest and understand.

Think Before You Speak

Saying the wrong thing at an inappropriate time can be quite embarrassing. That old saying is true, "You only get one time to make a first impression." Choose your words wisely. If you cannot think of anything that you are 100% sure is appropriate to say, do not say anything at all. Realize that words have different meanings according to the context in which they are used. Remember, words can easily offend if taken out of context. Leave no room for assumption or misunderstanding.

Be Clear and Confident

Focus on articulating your point of view and enunciating your words. Be certain to clearly express your thoughts, concerns, expectations and feelings. Be specific about how the issue or circumstance affects you personally. Be open to clarifying your ideas and be able to support your claims with proof. Listeners often lose patience with speakers who are vague, mumble or talk without a clear point. Do not beat around the bush.

- **Check Your Body Language**

    Since more than 90% of what is conveyed in face-to-face conversation has nothing to do with what is said, and more information is telegraphed by body language, it gives the strongest indication of what you are thinking. So, sit or stand up straight. Slouching shows a lack of confidence. Refrain from inappropriate gestures and facial expressions. Remember, that movements and gestures, like words, can be misinterpreted and can cause confusion.

    To appear your most confident, make eye contact. The inability to look a person in the eye gives the impression that you have something to hide or are immature. The goal is to show that you are interested in what the other person is saying, you are confident and you are capable of standing behind your words.

- **Speak Positively**

    Remove negative phrases from your day-to-day conversations. Phrases that begin with **barrier words** like "can't", "unable" and "won't" begin to work against your self-esteem by making you seem unable. Barrier words are also open to interpretation by the listener and may sound like your judgments.

    The use of **enabler words** like "can," "capable," "will," increase your self-esteem as words of accomplishment. Enabler words are positive and clear. They sound helpful and are viewed as encouraging. Using positive sentence construction emphasizes to the listener that a positive outcome can be expected.

- **Speak In a Pleasant Tone**

    Tone of voice also gives an indication of what you are feeling. "How you say it" is more important than what you say. Tone of voice and speech patterns can have make what you are attempting to say come out differently than you meant it.

    Voice inflection stresses what is important, so if used inappropriately it can lead to miscommunication. Likewise, pauses placed in the wrong locations may give the listener an opportunity to interrupt before you complete your thought. Make sure that your tone of voice echoes your mood. In general, speak in a pleasant tone and refrain from shouting or mouthing your words.

- **Identify Issues Quickly**

    The easiest problem to solve is the problem that has been identified, so identify issues quickly and bring them forward for discussion. Handle issues as soon as they arise. Small problems that are not identified and discussed early can become huge issues later.

    Enlist the aid of others to help you solve issues if necessary. If you don't know how to resolve an issue, find someone who does. Be respectful and gracious when providing or receiving feedback. Remember, without feedback there is no improvement.

- **Be Assertive and Passionate**

    Assertiveness is thoughtful and well-planned persistence toward persuading someone to adopt your point of view. Be assertive and passionate but not aggressive in what you are discussing. Aggression is an overbearing, win at all cost mentality, which often overlooks vital details (Bower, 1991). Most people merely shut down and refuse to "play along" when the other party is being aggressive. The listener may discount what you are saying if you come on too strong. Stand up for what you believe in. Let the listener hear your conviction in your words without being boisterous.

- **Focus on the Cause**

    Do not blame or focus on who is at fault. Instead turn the attention on what you and the listener can do to change the outcome of the situation by focusing on the issue and its solution. Focus on the root cause of the problem or the issues.

- **Reflect on the Conversation**

    Review the conversation and determine what could have been said differently. Focus on what words, if properly selected, would have provided your expected outcome. Use that lesson, moving forward.

QUESTIONNAIRE

Answer the following questions:

1. Name two ways of communicating?
   _____
   _____
   _____
   _____

2. Can you use more than one way of communicating at any given time?
   _____
   _____
   _____
   _____

3. How can you confuse others with your communication?
   _____
   _____
   _____
   _____

4. How can you effectively communicate?
   _____
   _____
   _____
   _____

Section 10: Motivation

A key to understanding how to overcome the struggle you face in reaching your potential, is to know what your needs are and what motivates you. In the section below, we will discuss in great detail what the most common needs are and how the needs affect our behavior. Be sure to pay special attention to both the positive aspects (how they work in positive ways) and their negative aspects (how people use more forceful or destructive ways to get their needs met) and then identify your needs.

The Nine Needs:

Each of us has three primary needs and six secondary needs. The hierarchy of needs is different for each of us. When people do not get their needs met, they can become agitated, belligerent or driven to use negative behaviors to see to it that their needs are met (*The Nine*, 1997).

Eventually, parents step aside and each person becomes responsible for seeing that they get their own needs met. Making sure you have everything you need is personal and it starts from the inside out. Most of these essentials cannot be fulfilled by another person. However, a group of needs can be shared. Most of the people you are close to, such as your friends, teammates, and band mates, share the same needs with you. The ability to share needs creates a deep connection or common bond. Close friends will usually share two or three needs in common. Conversely, people with whom you have little to no bond will fail to share at least one of your needs (*The Nine*, 1997).

1) Security

Security is the need to feel safe. It is the confidence that you are covered regardless of the circumstances. It is the feeling of assurance we get when we know what is going to happen and we know ahead of time what our plans are. It is the need to be in a familiar place, surrounded by familiar people. Security is the feeling of being protected. The ways we express the need for security vary from person to person. Here are some examples of how some people communicate the need for security (*The Nine*, 1997). See if you can identify with any of the items listed:

Expression of Security	**Protection From**
Having lots of money	Poverty, lack or worry
Having a boy or girl friend	Loneliness
Attending a party with several of your friends	Having to struggle by yourself
Having a dependable car	Rejection
Living near friends and family	Being stranded or being late to work

<u>Positive aspects:</u> The need for security keeps us balanced and grounded. It prevents us from taking unnecessary risks. It keeps us connected to family and friends. Helps us develop new relationships, networks and allows us to trust other people. The need for security drives self-confidence and the ability to make things happen. It gives us hope that everything will be okay in our lives.

Negative aspects: The need for security may make you overly cautious and fearful of risk. It may paralyze you and hinder you from making decisions. The inability to make decisions may cost you an opportunity. The need for security may lead you to take a defensive posture. It can cause you to retaliate against someone who you believe will destroy your sense of security.

2) Power

People with a need for power need to be in a position of influence and responsibility. The need for power pushes us to accomplish tasks and develop a reputation for succeeding in getting things done (*The Nine*, 1997). Some examples that satisfy the need for power are:

- Becoming a leader on a sports team or in an organization
- Achieving success
- Helping others feel empowered
- Becoming an authority on some topic
- Taking on responsibility for things, projects, events, situations
- Taking charge during an emergency or crisis

Positive aspects: The need for power may cause you to be more organized, precise and mindful of responsibility. The need for power develops leadership and self-empowerment skills. It leverages accomplishments to gain influence.

Negative aspects: The need for power may cause you to abuse relationships. It may also cause you to use deceit and manipulation to gain more control. The need for power, if used inappropriately, can cause you to commit acts of anger, lust and violence against others or things.

3) Adventure

Adventure is the need to try something new, fresh or exciting. It is the need to be first, to conquer or to discover. It is the need behind the motivation to travel, to explore and experience cultures. Adventure drives the notion of "getting the most out of life" and is intrigued by the sense of anticipation about upcoming events (The Nine, 1997). The need for adventure can take the form of:

- Planning new trips (even if they are never taken)
- Changing friends or love interest
- Changing jobs frequently
- Moving frequently
- Buying a new car every year
- Being an entrepreneur or being self-employed
- Conquering something (climbing the highest mountain, winning the gold medal, setting new records)

Positive aspects: The need for adventure challenges us to build on our past accomplishments. It drives innovation by forcing us to find new inventive ways of doing things. The need for adventure dares us to take risks and investigate opportunities. Adventure projects higher self-confidence, independence, optimism, excitement and enthusiasm for living.

Negative aspects: The need for adventure may cause

you to indulge in reckless and irresponsible behavior. It can cause you to disregard or bypass warnings as an excuse for excitement. The need for adventure may cause you to instigate fights or engage in foolish feats or challenges to satisfy your need for exhilaration. The need for adventure may cause you to gamble.

4) Freedom

Freedom is the need for autonomy and spontaneity. It is the feeling of independence. Freedom is the notion that you can do whatever you want, when you want to do it. It is also the need to be "free" to make your own choices and decisions. Freedom is impulsive and enjoys changing plans on a whim. The need for freedom prefers flexibility and is hampered by strict authority and heavy organizational structure. Here are some examples of how some people express the need for freedom (*The Nine,* 1997).

- Feeling free of restrictions
- Saying whatever comes to mind
- Making choices about relationships
- Refusing to obey rules that were created by someone else
- Changing appearance, hair style or way of dressing
- Getting piercings and tattoos
- Feeling free to be themselves, regardless of what they are doing or what situation they find themselves in
- Refusing to make and stick to decisions

<u>Positive aspects:</u> The need for freedom forces us to do things on our own. It allows us to discover new tastes

and experiences. It permits us to explore our thoughts and break away from norms to follow our dreams. The need for freedom builds self-confidence and high self-esteem.

Negative aspects: The need for freedom can prevent you from asking questions when you need help. It can also cause you to alienate friends by changing plans at the last minute. It can stop you from committing to a long-term plan.

5) Exchange

Exchange is the need to trade valuable commodities with others. The commodities can be information, conversation, friendship, services or money. It is also the need to exchange gifts, love, justice, or share experiences. It is the need to barter, trade, delegate, and enlist others to help problem solve (*The Nine*, 1997). Here are some examples of how some people express this need:

- Participating with others in discussions of all types
- Team work
- Educating yourself and teaching others
- Feeling a sense of integrity and trust with others
- Sharing information with others and receiving information in return
- Sharing a deep relationship with another person, where they feel able to communicate and interact freely and easily

Positive aspects: The need to exchange helps you support good relationships by allowing the flow of valuable information. It permits you to barter and trade goods and services to get you closer to reaching your goals.

<u>Negative aspects:</u> The need to exchange information may cause you to withhold information in favor of trading for a better commodity. You may engage in gossip, lying and criticism. The need for exchange may permit you to participate in unjust and unethical behavior in the treatment of others.

6) **Improvement and Expansion**

The need for improvement and expansion is categorized by the call to build or create something. It is the need to add to, to make better or to grow. It allows us to expand our horizons and to push the envelope of discovery. The need for improvement and expansion shifts boundaries, presses limits and increases capacity as we strive for success (*The Nine*, 1997). Examples include:

- Creating a personal fortune
- Expanding a collection of any kind
- Discovering new ways of doing things
- Becoming a real estate developer
- Moving to a bigger home
- Seeing the bigger picture

<u>Positive aspects:</u> The need for expansion may cause you to want to learn a new skill or attempt a new sport. It may also cause you to explore ideas and master new interests. It will lead you to investigate and understand how the world works. The need for expansion will help

you develop the processes of self-assessment, discovery, and improvement. It helps you view opportunities based on your available resources and assists in obtaining the tools necessary to effectively plan to reach your goals.

Negative aspects: The need for improvement and expansion may cause you to hoard items that you may not need. It can also drive you to attempt to grow and mature too quickly. The need for improvement and expansion can also be a distraction and focus your attention on the next revolutionary idea rather than on simple solutions to problems.

7) **Acceptance**

Acceptance is the need to acknowledge your own thoughts, feelings and emotions as well as to be accepted by others. This includes a feeling of belonging. It is also the need to accept others (*The Nine*, 1997). Examples of how this need is expressed:
- Participating in situations that are open and accepting of everyone
- Being accepted as a valuable member of a family group
- Belonging to a club, group or team
- Feeling loved
- Accepting whatever comes up in life
- Doing things that make others feel good
- Being nice regardless of the situation or the person
- Being tolerant of self and others

Positive aspects: The need to be accepted helps you to

create valuable relationships. It also helps you understand why you feel the way you feel and encourages self-esteem, self-forgiveness, and forgiveness of others. It helps us empathize with others. It also makes us good and unselfish teammates.

<u>Negative aspects:</u> The need for acceptance can become an obsession. Wanting people to like you may cause you to conform. If used inappropriately, you can use the need for acceptance to reject others and to develop jealousy and prejudice.

8) **Expression**

Expression is the need to communicate your thoughts artistically. It is the need to be seen, to be heard, and to be felt. It is the need to convey who we are through words, speech, actions, dress, and art (*The Nine*, 1997). Here are some examples of expression:

- Creating and publishing daily blogs
- Writing books, poems, articles and journals
- Unique tattoos and piercings
- Painting
- Dancing or acting

<u>Positive aspects:</u> The need for expression allows you to demonstrate individual talent and creativity. It permits you to communicate effectively and keeps your emotions in balance. It promotes understanding of yourself and others through art, words and behavior.

<u>Negative aspects:</u> The need for expression may cause you to express yourself inappropriately or at the wrong time

causing an invasion of other's space. The need to express something may prompt you to create a false image to outwardly express. It may also cause you to be less willing to allow others to express themselves, especially if you do not agree with what they are communicating.

9) Community

Community is the need to be in the midst of or surrounded by large groups of people. The need for community places the needs of others in high regard. This need seeks out people and is able to maintain large numbers of relationships. The need for community is different from the need for exchange in that the need for community does not require anything to be traded (*The Nine*, 1997).

Here are some of the ways people express the need for community:

- Throwing parties for the slightest of reasons
- Participating in classes, groups and clubs
- Volunteering at social functions
- Starting and participating in online chat rooms
- Hosting family gatherings and groups of friends
- Running for public office
- Gathering signatures for a petition or a ballot initiative

Positive aspects: The need for community allows you to gain friends and influence people through acts of service. It is essential in developing your networking skills. It creates a sense of your own importance and dignity in relation to the rest of humanity.

<u>Negative aspects:</u> The need for community can be a distraction in part because of always wanting people around. You may choose to throw a party instead of studying (such behavior would be irresponsible). It may also cause you to become needy because of wanting to have constant contact.

Motivation

The basis of every motivation is a need. Think about it, if you are motivated to play the latest video game, what is driving you to play? Is it because you want to be the first to play the game? Was it to escape to a different world? Was it to conquer each challenge or to win a contest? As we discussed earlier, it is clear to see that each of these responses can be traced back to an essential need. Motivation, then, is strength of the desire to supply your need. It is the vehicle that turns the desire to secure wants into the realization of obtaining those wants. Motivation is rooted in our aspiration to minimize loss and maximize rewards.

Motivation also balances needs against your moral values. If you want to go to college, for example, you may be motivated to study or cheat, depending on your personal values, in order to pass your classes. Likewise, if you were hungry would you resort to stealing to satisfy your need? Success demands that you are motivated to work toward your goal. The key is to be motivated for the right reasons and to allow the positive aspects of the "need," we discussed earlier, to dominate your personality.

A simple test to find out what is motivating you to do something is to ask yourself why you are doing it. Typically, within the first 5 whys, you have reached the root cause of your motivation. Here is a simple example to illustrate:

I am motivated to exercise every day. Why?
I want to live a healthy life. Why?
I want a more attractive body. Why?
I hate the way I look? Why?
I want to look more attractive. Why?
So, I will be accepted

As we mature, our motivation may change, but the need we are driven to satisfy, will stay the same. For example, if the need is to be accepted, the motivation to exercise daily may be replaced by the desire to work hard on your job. In the next section, we will discuss the types of motivation that you may encounter. As you read them, think of a goal you want to achieve. Identify what your motivation is as well as the type. Then, think about what need your motivation is fulfilling.

Types of Motivation

Achievement Motivation

It is the drive to pursue and attain goals. If you are motivated by achievement, you will wish to **achieve** objectives and advance up on the ladder of success. Here, your accomplishment is important for its own sake and not for any of the associated rewards that accompany it (Mussieux, n.d.).

Affiliation Motivation

It is a drive to connect to people on a social level. If you are motivated by affiliation, you will work better when you are complimented for your demeanor and attitude of co-operation (Mussieux, n.d.).

Competence Motivation

It is the drive to be great at something. It is the pursuit to consistently perform at a high level. If you are motivated by competency, you will seek job mastery and take pride in developing and using your problem-solving skills. You will strive to be creative when confronted with problems and barriers. You will also learn from their experience (Mussieux, n.d.).

Power Motivation

It is the drive to influence people and change situations. If you are motivated by power, you will wish to create an impact on the lives of your friends and your organization and you are willing to take risks to do so (Mussieux,n.d.).

Attitude Motivation

It is the determination to make decisions based on how you think and feel. It is your attitude toward life, your belief in yourself and your self-confidence. It is how you feel about the future and how you react to the past (Mussieux, n.d.).

QUESTIONNAIRE

Answer the following questions:

1. What are the nine human needs?

   _____
   _____
   _____
   _____

2. What is the positive aspect of the Security need?

   _____
   _____
   _____

3. What is the negative aspect of the Adventure need?

   _____
   _____
   _____
   _____

4. Give a recent example of how you positively fulfilled the need of acceptance. Comment on the result.

   _____
   _____
   _____
   _____

Motivation

5. Identify the five types of motivation.

_____

_____

_____

6. Which motivation style fits you?

_____

_____

_____

GAME ON: Tools and Strategies for Living on Purpose

Section 11: Foundations of Mentorship

In Greek mythology, Odysseus, king of Ithaca, a small Greek State, entrusted the care of his only son, Telemachus, to his close friend, **Mentor**, while he was away fighting in the Trojan War. News of Odysseus, cunningly devised schemes, victories, and triumphs made him legendary among the Greeks. His Trojan horse is credited as the decisive strategy of the Trojan War. Yet despite his victories on the battlefield, he encountered countless obstacles on the journey home from war (*What is a mentor*, 2013).

As the years passed, many soldiers began returning home from battle, but King Odysseus was not counted among them. Knowing that Odysseus' kingdom would be challenged while he was away, the Goddess Athena kept watch over Telemachus. When the beautiful goddess visited Telemachus, she disguised herself as Mentor to hide herself from the men who were attempting to "court" the Queen Penelope, overthrow the kingdom and kill Telemachus, the true king's only heir. As Mentor, the goddess encouraged Telemachus to stand up against those who challenged his father's rule and go abroad to find out what happened to his father. Odysseus and Telemachus returned to kill all of those who plotted against the kingdom (*What is a mentor*, 2013).

"Because of Mentor's relationship with Telemachus, and the disguised Athena's encouragement and practical plans for dealing with personal dilemmas, the personal name *Mentor* has been adopted in English as a term meaning someone who imparts wisdom to and shares knowledge with a less experienced colleague" (*What is a mentor,* 2013, para. 2),

As seen in this historical note above, there are many in the past that have profited from the help, support, example and advice of an older or more experienced person. Today, the super famous and ridiculously wealthy, such as Oprah Winfrey and Bill Gates, owe a portion of their tremendous success and great esteem to mentors (*Oprah and Bill,* March 2011). Mentoring can be seen in everyday life and even in pop-culture (i.e. Obi-wan Kenobi mentored Anakin Skywalker). We can see the benefits of walking with someone and learning from their advice and direction. This type of relationship can provide security and direction for the younger partner and can be very valuable by helping them progress much faster in their given pursuit.

What is a Mentor?

A mentor is someone, usually older, more knowledgeable or more experienced, who can provide wisdom, guidance or direction to an inexperienced person. The person who is mentored is typically called the **mentee**. The mentee draws from the information provided by the mentor and makes a conscious decision to heed and act on the mentor's advice. Although this type of relationship seems one sided, it can be mutually beneficial. The mentor is able to pass on valuable life lessons they have learned and gain the sense of accomplishment by helping someone else succeed. The mentee can benefit from the knowledge, direction and support passed on from the mentor in the areas of career development, personal relationships, hobbies, etc.

In order for the mentoring relationship to work, the mentor must be someone who understands the needs of the mentee. They must understand the mentee's current situation and be able to create a roadmap for the mentee to reach goals and paint a picture for eventual success. A mentor's past experiences and practical knowledge is valuable information to the mentee. This type of knowledge is not based on guess work, or wishful thinking. Instead, a mentor's input is based on the understanding of someone who has gone where the mentee wishes to go and has encountered and overcome the barriers that the mentee may face.

Role Models and Mentors

While both role models and mentors are needed to be successful, the two should not be confused. As we have discussed throughout the program, role models can be anyone: alive or dead; people you know or don't; or folks that you have seen or read about that can be viewed as an example. They may have particular behaviors and skills that we may wish to imitate, but we may not have any personal contact with them. Role models provide illustrations of what is possible to achieve with very little insight or personal dialogue on to how to bring the illustrations to pass. In other words, they provide inspiration by what they represent.

On the other hand, a mentor is someone who is living and is willing to develop a relationship with you. They will take the time to get to know you and your current situation. They allow you access to them and, in some cases, their personal and professional networks. Mentors may have insight into what you are feeling and use dialogue, activities, and exercises to equip you with tools to develop your character and help you cope. They can provide you with valuable feedback and direct input on your current situations to perfect your talents and focus your aspirations. Most of all, they can provide personal encouragement and help boost enthusiasm. A mentor can be seen as a role model if they exhibit a certain quality you wish to adopt but they serve a different purpose. We are not down playing the purpose of a role model; we are just illustrating the difference. Take a look at the following example:

Tiger Woods is a role model for developing the perfect golf swing. However, if you attempt to call Tiger and talk to him about helping your swing, you may not get the results you are looking for. Why? He may not be willing to share his opinion with you because there is no tangible relationship. He knows nothing about your swing and may not care enough to help you fix it. On the other hand, if you seek out a person at the community center, at school or in church, they may take a vested interest in helping to develop your golf game.

Why Mentors Are Invaluable

While role models provide motivation by what they symbolize, mentors provide encouragement, motivation and practical wisdom through personal relationship. Think back to when you were learning algebra. For every lesson in the book, there was a set of examples; some were derivations and others were proofs. Yet, for all the information provided in each example, the examples were silent on what exactly you were doing wrong. Conversely, a mentor, in this case a coach or teacher, was able to accurately diagnose where you had difficulty and provided learning strategies that were tailored to your specific learning style. In the section below, we will discuss common benefits of having access to a mentor to coach you through life's situations.

Barrier and Pitfall Elimination

There are many barriers, pitfalls and traps that can threaten a student's future success. A mentor can steer the mentee away from these setbacks, help prevent errors and assist mentees in staying focused on what is important. They can share with the mentee mistakes they have made in the past and warn them of approaching dangers. They may also have an extensive network of people who can be called upon to remove barriers and provide specific, area focused insight and support to solve problems.

Think of a mentor as a quarterback who is aware of the running back's goal of successfully running through a hole created by the offensive line. If the quarterback sees the defense bringing another defender to the line to prevent the running back from reaching his goal, he can call an audible. An audible is a loud signal that changes the play. The quarterback can reposition players to support the goal of the running back. In this case, a quarterback may call for an offensive lineman to pull and motion a full back into position to block the additional defenders and remove the impending threat to the running back.

Guidance and Direction

As you mature, you will face several life changing decisions. New ideas and opportunities will continue to pop up and attempting to find your own way can be risky and time consuming. External pressures, thoughts and opinions will never be in short supply and knowing which road to take, how to get started, and who to talk to may be difficult at times. Finding the right opportunities that align with your goals may also be difficult to distinguish. Having a person in your corner that understands the odds, has perspective on what is at stake, and has the expertise in your area of interest is precious. Mentors can help the mentee figure out the next step to take, the direction and speed in which to move, and can provide support to help the mentee accomplish goals.

Person Growth

As mentioned in previous sections of this book, it is important to have the input of others because we may not see everything happening around us or in us. Even if your head were on a swivel and you had a 360 degree vantage point, your perception of unfolding events may be skewed. We may not always see or be willing to acknowledge what our flaws or weaknesses are. Talking to a mentor can provide a clear perspective and help us focus on becoming better students, better employees and, ultimately, better people. For example, are you monotone during your presentations? Do you display confidence with others? Do you have major character flaws such as being quick tempered or being too sharp with your words? Even if you identify these issues in yourself, how do you resolve them? What is the next step? Whom do you consult? A mentor can not only help you identify these problems, but also can provide help on how to resolve them.

Finding a Mentor

Before gaining the benefits having a mentor can

provide, it is crucial that you find a mentor that can meet your needs. It is good to have an idea of what you are looking for. In this section, we will discuss the critical steps to locating a mentor. You will notice a few similarities to finding a role model with minor changes. Take a moment to identify the steps that you have already taken or will need to take.

Identify and Review your Goals

Take a moment to review your short and long term goals. Are you aware of what is next? What type of help will you need to meet your goals? Think about what tasks you will have to complete and which actions steps will be the most challenging. If you are considering, career goals, for example, be sure to include your educational and personal desires. Practice writing your goals down and spend time talking about the goals you wish to accomplish. Capture your goals and questions on paper to share with perspective mentors. Be very specific about what you want to do and highlight your goals for the mentoring relationship.

Establish Your Criteria

Once you have identified your goals, highlight a list of the attributes you think your mentor should have. Be specific about type of personality, background and communication style you are looking for. A person's external attributes, such as race, gender, wealth and level of education, do not matter as much as them having a genuine concern for your future and a desire to spend their time with you to help you progress. Leave some room for flexibility; sometimes great gifts come in packages we don't expect.

Network with and Interview Family and Friends

The best place to start is with people you know, family members, teachers or employers. You can also ask them if they know someone who is currently advancing towards or has achieved the same goals you are attempting to reach. Do not be afraid to ask around and see who could fit the mold for you. The goal, again, is to find someone who is willing to give of their time to understand you and give you input on reaching your goals.

Identify Candidates and Ask for Their Help

Once you have a list of people your relatives and friends or employers recommend, refer back to your criteria. Spend some time thinking about who has the skills you want to possess or has reached the level of performance that you want to attain. Develop a short questionnaire to pinpoint the professional and personality traits that you want to acquire. Ask your friends and loved ones to make the initial connection for you and strike up a conversation. A face to face meeting with the connector and the proposed mentor in a public place works best. However, telephone conversations may be all that is required. Observe the natural flow of the conversation and make note of the positive and negative "vibes" that you receive when asking the questions on your list.

Find a Person You Can Relate To

An ideal mentor is someone you can relate to and who also relates to you. As with all relationships, a mentoring relationship will not last long if you cannot communicate with your mentor or they are unable to speak to you in ways that you will understand. Likewise, you will find it difficult to carry out their advice if you cannot trust that what they are telling you is in your best interest. You must find a person whose advice you will follow. You must be able and willing to put what is discussed into practice. Consider finding a mentor who has been in your current situation in the past or one that is in the situation you desire to grow to. Remember, have some flexibility; the goal is to find someone you can talk with who can empathize with you.

Be Prepared and Keep an Opened Mind

As stated in the beginning of the chapter, a mentor's job is to help assess your potential and help you devise a plan to realize it. In doing so, they may ask you to change your behavior, adopt new habits, or elevate your thinking. They may also expose you to new educational experiences in various professional settings. You may not always see the relevance of each task or experience to your situation at first but go with the flow. Remember, a diamond must be cut, shaped, polished and refined to reveal its true brilliance. Be open- minded and take good notes. Be sure that you enter you relationship with the end in mind; reaching your goals. Start down the road of revealing your brilliance.

Be Assertive
Continue to call and schedule appointments with your mentor. Keep in contact with them and keep them up to speed on everything that is going on. Provide feedback on what you learned by applying what they have taught you. Above all else, be a sponge; soak up any and everything your mentor has to say, figure out how to apply it, and act accordingly on what is said.

Tips on Being Mentored

<u>Develop a Good Relationship</u>. Remember that mentoring relationships require input from the mentor and the mentee. Mentoring relationships are built on trust. It is important that you are open and honest with your mentor about what your needs are. Do not be afraid to reach out to them. Building good relationships takes effort.

<u>Contribute to the Conversation</u>. It is best to come to any time you have together prepared. Think ahead about what direction you need and what questions you would like to ask. Come to your time together with pen and paper ready to write down any insights and advice given. If you have questions about anything discussed, don't be too proud to ask for clarification. If there are any specific actions that you need to take, make sure you review them with your mentor before your time ends.

<u>Place Plans into Action</u>. After your meeting, be diligent to put their input into practice. A mentor will not be satisfied with you taking their precious time and not following through on what was discussed.

<u>Develop a Schedule.</u> It is also good to settle on how often you would like to meet and prioritize which goals you aim to achieve. This will keep you on task, help you to see your progress and be an encouragement to you and your mentor.

<u>The More, the Merrier</u>. No one person is an expert in everything. A basketball coach, for example, may not be the best choice for helping you develop a financial plan. The

coach's expertise is basketball. For financial planning, you may choose a businessperson, an investor or an accountant unless the coach is also a financial wiz. Likewise, you may choose to have a mentor for every facet of your life.

<u>Build in Some Flexibility</u>. Your mentor may change over time due to several factors: you or your mentor may move, time constraints may prohibit routine meetings, your goals may change or you may out-grow their expertise. If you are separated from your mentor, continue to search for another. Remember your goal is to keep growing.

<u>Be Appreciative and Respectful</u>. Always be appreciative of what they are able to offer you and be respectful, even in the times that you disagree with their input. Ultimately, the decision to place what you have learned into action rests with you. If you feel what they are telling you is not in your best interest, thank them for their input and humbly explain your decision to move in a different direction.

<u>Change if it is Not Working</u>. Do not view your meeting with your mentor as a necessary or evil thing. Nor should your meeting be seen as a chore that must be performed to satisfy a "success checklist." Instead, it should be viewed as an informal, beneficial conversation where you are free to ask questions and have your needs met. If you find, however, that it is difficult to communicate with or spend time with your mentor, or if your progress has stalled out, do not be afraid to find another mentor in that area.

QUESTIONNAIRE

Answer the following questions:

1) Why is it important to have a mentor?
_____
_____
_____

2) How does having a mentor differ from a having a role model?
_____
_____
_____

3) How can you go about selecting a mentor?
_____
_____
_____

4) What things would you talk to your mentor about?
_____
_____
_____

Section 12: Conflict Management

No leadership model exists that will totally eliminate miscommunication or clashes of personality. Disagreements and misunderstandings occur. Conflict is a part of life. There is no way of getting around it. As you mature, you can be sure that you'll face conflicts. In fact, the tension that comes from conflict can be healthy and beneficial to personal growth, if dealt with correctly. Because conflict is inevitable, you must learn how to manage your responses and work through the conflict constructively.

One of the major responses to the pressure associated with conflict is to get angry. Understanding this, and learning to control your anger is one of the first steps to successfully managing conflict.

Anger

From time to time we all get upset. Whether it is being "disrespected" in our neighborhood or feeling like we are not being "heard" at home, we all get angry. Anger is as natural an emotion as love or fear. Anger is our emotional response to displeasure, feeling threatened or not having our needs and expectations met. Anger happens when we think our emotional, psychological, physical or social well-being is challenged. It can be the product of unresolved issues and problems, unfair criticism, lack of communication or a feeling that there has been an injustice. Anger can also result from verbal or physical threats, frustration or disappointment.

If left unchecked, anger can be a distraction and carry serious consequences. It can pre-occupy us with attempting to identify who is at fault, attaching blame, or with aggressively defending our position. Rather than attempting to resolve the issue, or manage the conflict, anger focuses our thoughts on resentment and "pay back." Our resentment may be fed by jealousy, irritability or rejection. Uncontrolled anger leads to rage and eventually maybe even hatred; causing us to lash out in negative behavior that may result in verbal abuse, damage to property or bodily harm to yourself and others.

In fact, the destructive impacts of anger can be seen all around us. We cannot log onto the Internet, pick up a newspaper or turn on the television without seeing news of crimes that can be directly related to anger. We even encounter enraged people on our roads. In some cases, we are confronted with the devastating effects of anger in our own homes, schools and neighborhoods. Consider the deadly attacks at Columbine High School in 1999, Red Lake High School in 2005 and Virginia Tech in 2007. How can people become so angry that they explode in such unbelievable acts of violence?

How can people become so vicious, so blind to right and wrong? Research has shown that the anger that causes horrifying events is not born overnight. Odds are it began with frustration and minor irritations, like the ones we all feel and experience daily. The difference is that the initial conflict was not resolved and the resulting anger was not appropriately expressed. Instead, the unresolved issues and the resulting frustration were allowed to fester, grow and spiral out of control.

Think of a recent situation where you over-reacted. Explain and describe the situation that made you angry and why?

_____
_____
_____

Explain and describe what you were thinking about in that situation? What thoughts went through your mind?

_____
_____
_____

Did your thoughts make you less angry? Or, more angry?

_____

What did you say or do in that instant?

_____
_____
_____

Describe the results of your actions?

_____
_____

Describe what you could have done differently to change your anger reaction into a different one?

_____
_____

Glancing back now, can you think of a better way in which you could have handled the situation?

_____

_____

Common Myths about Anger

In order to understand and control our anger, we must review and understand some common misconceptions about anger. The most common myths regarding anger are:

<u>All anger is dangerous</u>. Anger can be dangerous, but it can have positive attributes as well. It can motivate us to achieve. Anger and outrage can also motivate change. When it is used properly, anger can be used to communicate effectively and solve problems. For example, our nation was outraged over the government's slow response to the food and water crisis caused by Hurricane Katrina. Anger over the perceived injustice united compassionate people to act. People in huge numbers volunteered and sent food, water and finances to aid the region after the floods.

<u>Being angry is unhealthy</u>. While it is true that uncontrolled anger can lead to stress related health issues, anger itself is not unhealthy. A properly balanced and controlled expression of how you feel is healthy. To suppress your feelings or to imagine they do not exist will only cause problems down the road. Feelings that are not dealt with early may explode into physical and emotional problems later. If we learn to control our expression of thoughts, feelings and behaviors, anger will have no effect on our health.

<u>You have no control of your anger</u>. Anger is based on our perception of a situation and is greatly influenced by our thoughts. That means we can **choose** to allow our thoughts to either increase or decrease the level of our responses to situations. For example, if you focus long enough on a time when a loved one let you down, sooner or later you will remember more instances when they failed to meet your expectations. The more you dwell on your loved one's past failures the more frustrated you will become with the current situation and the angrier you will be. We can change the way we think and feel about situations, objects and people. That means we can control whether or not we get angry. Therefore, no one can make us angry without our permission.

<u>Controlling your anger.</u> Most people handle anger in three major ways. They 1) express it, 2) suppress it, or 3) transform it. Appropriately expressing anger means saying how you feel, using the effective communication tools you learned in previous sections. It also means working through the conflict rationally.

On the other hand, expressing anger inappropriately includes starting a fight, damaging property, verbally assaulting someone, gossiping or transferring blame. Inappropriately expressing anger, or even suppressing anger, become habits and lead to anger management issues as you go on. Suppressing your feelings of anger can cause withdrawal, hatred and guilt. It may also cause health-related risks. Transforming your anger involves using anger management techniques whenever possible to resolve the issue and remain calm while doing so.

Transforming your anger into more productive energy may also include activities that allow you to release that energy, such as taking up a new sport– or finding a creative outlet for stress and aggression in a new hobby.

Regardless of your age, you will have to develop a unique way to deal with your natural feelings of anger. In order to be successful, you will want to follow a program that will allow you to channel your anger and aggression positively.

Here are a few simple suggestions of things you can do to control your anger:

<u>Recognize whether or not you have an anger problem.</u> One clear-cut sign that you have a problem with anger management is the inability to "let it go." Anger consumes you when you get mad about something and regardless of the fact that it's getting better, you tend to stay angry about it for a long time. You may express your anger often, or just keep it inside and hold a grudge against the person you are upset with. You should recognize that this can be very damaging to your quality of life. Holding grudges weighs you down with hatred, and all aspects of your life are caught up in the negative effects of your prolonged anger. Change the things you cannot deal with. Recognize that there are things you cannot change - and let them go.

<u>Do not suppress your anger.</u> Think of anger as a weed seed. Like many other emotions, it grows inside of you as you "fertilize" it with energy and focus. A seed that has just been planted is easily removed, but as time passes, the seed becomes harder to remove because it sprouts roots that dig in deep. Eventually, it will take a lot of effort to remove the weed that resulted from the seed. Instead, respectfully express your anger. If you cannot verbalize how you feel, write your feelings and emotions in a journal or find

another outlet.

Learn more about what "sets you off." Perform a self-assessment and think about the types of situations and events that make you angry. Think about why the events upset you and attempt to solve the issues that you know trigger your anger. If you are unable to handle the situation without acting in a way that is negative, remove yourself from the situation or conversation and only return once you have calmed down.

Relax and restructure your thinking. Remind yourself that getting angry is not going to solve your problems. Too many people abandon logic when they are emotionally charged, angry or confused. A level head is needed to communicate, solve problems and avoid dangerous situations.

- Do not make assumptions or act on assumptions. Understand that you may not be thinking clearly and the circumstance may not be as it seems.
- If the situation is as you perceive it, remind yourself that every problem has a solution.
- Remember, you control your thoughts and your thoughts control your emotions.

Learn to control your emotions and delay your response. It is so important to remain calm and respectful, even if the other person involved in the conflict is not. There's an old saying: "Life is 10% what happens to you and 90% how you react to it." You choose 90% of the event by choosing how to react. The situation could escalate quickly and spiral out of control if you act too soon or on wrong information.

- Learn to respect the other person's point of view. Listen empathetically, with heart, and do not take what the other person is saying personally.
- Take a deep breath. If necessary count to ten, then think about the best way to act. If the action is appropriate, do it - if not think of an alternative.
- Do not use what the other person says and feels as ammunition to fire back. When a person shares what they are really thinking and feeling, they are vulnerable for attack. To attack the other person when they are vulnerable may seem like a good strategy, but attacks of this type cause resentment and may escalate to physical violence.
- Remember most people just want to feel that they are being "heard." Most people typically calm down once they blow off a little steam.

<u>Find another outlet for your aggression</u>. Finding another outlet for your aggression and built-up frustration is one of the best, healthiest ways of working through your emotions. If you feel you must do something with your hands, consider that new sport or hobby.

Methods of Conflict Resolution

Now that we have taken a close look at anger and how to control it, let's take a look at the common methods of conflict resolution. Based on how we have been raised and our past experiences, we have learned several different methods for resolving conflicts. Many of those methods are ineffective and should be discarded. The key is to understand which methods are beneficial and become used to using these techniques. The goal is to resolve conflicts so that your relationships are left intact and that you both maintain your dignity and your integrity. Methods of conflict resolution include:

1) Win

The focus here is to end the day as the winner of the conflict. This is like kids on the playground playing "King of the Hill," where the last one standing wins. The desire to win, "at all costs," means you will manipulate, deceive, harm and destroy the person you are in conflict with. When you do this, you are not valuing the other person and their point of view, but just seeing them as an opponent to be defeated.

2) Run

This method is used when you desire to avoid the conflict out of fear or laziness. This is like someone putting on headphones, turning up the music or leaving the room to block out and avoid working through the issue at hand. The conflict still exists, but has been buried only to awaken again at another time.

3) Quit

Often in a desire to appease the other person in a conflict, you may decide to give in and allow them to win the day. You may still inwardly disagree with them, but giving them the victory will allow them a sense of satisfaction. But it isn't productive in building a strong and honest relationship. You just ... quit.

4) Compromise

In order to compromise, both parties must decide to "give a little in order to get a little." They will give in to some demand of the other person in order to get something for themselves. This method seems effective - but unless you truly understand the other person's point of view, these same issues can often come back up in future conflicts.

5) Resolve

Resolving the conflict requires both parties to talk through the issues so that the point of view and motivation of the other person is clearly understood. The conflict is resolved when the best solution for all parties is decided upon and implemented. Conflicts resolved in this manner rarely need to be revisited because the underlying issues have been dealt with.

Tips to Resolving Conflict

Conflict resolution is the best way to manage conflict. The trick is getting both parties to agree to start working through their issues of contention. Conflict resolution techniques are only really effective when both parties understand the consequences of not getting their needs met - and they wish to end the conflict without incident. For example, both you and a friend may desire to maintain the relationship and deal with your issues rather than continue to argue.

HINT: Tips that have been proven to work in resolving conflict include:

➤ **Develop a goal for the conversation.** Like "ground rules," it's good to know whether the goal is to heal the friendship, make peace and move past this relationship with no hard feelings, or get the credit you feel you deserve for your hard work on a project.

➤ **Determine your needs.** Understand what your limits are and decide what you are able to give up, if necessary, to resolve the issue.

➤ **Try not to get angry.** Anger can be a distraction and can cloud judgment. Issues can quickly escalate if you are not thinking clearly.

➤ **Try to work out misunderstandings as they occur.** Give the issue your undivided attention as soon as it is detected. Unresolved issues can grow into larger conflicts. If an apology is in order, be sincere, speak specifically about the offense and show that you understand why the person feels the way they feel.

➤ **Get help if necessary.** If either party is unwilling or unable to handle the issue appropriately, bring in a third party who is responsible and who you both can trust and respect.

➤ **Use truth and logic to accurately define the problem.** Gather as much information about the specifics of the issue as you can. Ask open-ended questions to "drill down" to the core of the primary cause of the complaint. Refocus the conversation if the subject or topic veers off course.

➤ **Listen more than you speak.** Do not assume anything. Allow the other individual to think and speak for themselves. Concentrate on listening and then clearly communicating your own thoughts. Lay your own negative perceptions and prejudices aside. A biased opinion is a worthless opinion. Use active listening techniques to empathize with the speaker.

➤ **Use effective communication techniques and maintain focus on the "workable" issues.** Use positive sentence construction, focusing on what is possible, to reassure the other person(s) that you are interested in resolving the conflict fairly.

➤ **Let them know where you're "coming from."** Be sure to communicate how the conflict personally affects you – so they will know what you feel and why you feel that way.

➤ **Handle only one issue at a time.** Trying to discuss or resolve more than one issue at a time can be a distraction. More often than not, one or both parties will become confused and misunderstandings will occur. Resolve one issue at a time. Re-state the resolution as necessary to prevent confusion and revisiting the issue.

➤ **Focus on the big picture and not just the conflict at hand.** Sometimes you may have to take a step back in order to take a step forward. Take a look at your final destination and decide how important engaging in a conflict is. If the consequences outweigh the rewards, agree to disagree and keep moving forward.

➤ **Resolve the issue by doing what is best for everyone, not just what is easiest.** Often compromise and negotiation are the only ways to resolve differences of opinion and clashes of personality. Reaching a fair compromise may take time. Taking the easiest option may prove to be unsatisfactory and cause further conflict. Review all the options and make sure that you agree with the negotiated solution.

➤ Do not allow conflict to undermine your plans and goals, ruin your attitude or demean your character. Conflict and controversy are stepping stones to reaching our goals. Learn to be assertive. Effectively manage the conflict and resist the temptation to abandon your dreams. Roll up your sleeves, reach out and take hold of your dreams.

Develop your own rules of engaging in conflict, decide which tips to adopt and control your anger. Practice daily. Soon you will notice that managing conflict is not as difficult as it sounds.

Everyone is not going to be thrilled with the way you think, how you choose to express yourself, how you behave or how successful you are. There will be people who will attempt to bait you into a fight or a verbal altercation just to show you that they can. Do not fall into that trap. Remind yourself of your goals and keep taking steps forward. What do you have to prove to them?

Remember, sometimes the path to success is a lonely path. You cannot control everyone else's thoughts or emotions. You can only control and communicate your own. While conflict is inevitable, you cannot allow adversity to ground your dreams before they take off. Instead, manage the adversity, overcome discord and allow your dreams to soar.

QUESTIONNAIRE

Answer the following questions:

1. What methods do you normally use to manage conflict?

_____

_____

_____

2. Have those methods always been effective for you?

_____

_____

3. What conflict(s) are you facing currently?

_____

_____

_____

4. What method(s) should you use to resolve this conflict?

_____

_____

_____

Section 13: Assert Yourself

In the previous modules, we discussed accepted conflict resolution techniques. In order to put those skills to good use, you must be assertive. When you are assertive you have the ability to be direct, open and honest. Being assertive allows you to state your position boldly and positively without fear of retribution. Assertive people make the best choices for themselves, stand up for themselves and exercise their rights without denying the rights of others (Smith, 1975). Assertiveness increases your ability to reach your goals while maintaining your rights and dignity.

Assertiveness is quite natural for some, but for those who don't have the natural ability, it is a skill that can be learned. When you have this ability you notice that it greatly reduces the level of misunderstandings and conflict in your life. In this chapter we will discuss how to harness assertiveness to reach your dreams. We will review the differences between assertive and aggressive behavior, what your rights are, when to be assertive, barriers to being assertive, tips to becoming more assertive and the benefits of being assertive.

Assertion is not Aggression

"Assertion is sometimes confused with aggression. This is probably due to the fact that both types of behavior involve standing up for one's rights and expressing one's needs" (Scott,n.d.,para.2). Standing up for one's rights and expressing one's needs is where the similarities end. The two styles bring about very different results.

Assertion requires an individual to express themselves in ways that respect others. It allows one to assume the best about others, respect oneself and think of seeing things from someone else's point of view.

On the other hand, an individual behaving aggressively has the tendency to express themselves in ways that are disrespectful, manipulative, demeaning, and abusive. These individuals make negative assumptions about the motives of others and do not look at situations from another person's point of view at all. They want to win at the expense of others and create unnecessary conflict (*Assertiveness*, n.d.).

Assertion affects many areas of life. Assertive people have the tendency to have fewer conflicts when dealing with others, which often means much less stress in their lives. Their needs are met; therefore, they are apt to help others get their needs met also. Assertive leaders have more support in their relationships with people they lead (*Assertiveness*, n.d.).

On the other hand aggressive leaders alienate others and create unnecessary stress. Those on the receiving end of aggression feel attacked and often avoid the aggressive leaders whenever possible. Over time, people who behave aggressively have a series of failed relationships and have little support from the people they lead.

What would you do in this situation?

Someone cuts in front of you at the supermarket.

_____
_____
_____
_____

Would you assume they did it on purpose?
_____
_____
_____

Would you react with anger and confront them?
_____
_____

In an assertive way (respecting yourself and others) how could you address the issue of line cutting?
_____
_____
_____
_____

What would you do in this situation? (Pick one)

You have a friend, who can be long-winded, and she calls you to vent about her bad day. Unfortunately, you have a lot of work to do and don't have time to talk.

1. ___Would you become angry that she obviously doesn't respect your time, cut her off and sarcastically say, "Oh, get over it! I have my own problems!"

Or

2. ____ Would you listen for a minute or two and then compassionately say, "Wow, it sounds like you're having a tough day! I'd love to talk to you about it, but I don't have the time right now. Can we talk later tonight?"

How is the second response an example of being Assertive (respecting yourself and others)?

_____
_____
_____
_____

What are the benefits of assertiveness?

_____
_____
_____
_____

How does one become more assertive?

_____
_____
_____
_____

Understanding Your Rights

As we stated at the beginning of this chapter, assertive people have strength in their convictions, stand up for themselves and exercise their rights without denying the rights of others. In order to exercise your rights, you must first understand what your rights are. The following is a list of rights, (Smith, 2000) most scholars agree, is the foundation for being assertive:

1) You have the right to pursue success and become successful
2) You have the right to set your own expectations
3) You have the right to express your needs, thoughts and desires even if they do not make any sense to others
4) You have the right to say "NO" without giving an explanation or without feeling guilty
5) You have the right to make mistakes
6) You have the right to make your own decisions and cope with any associated consequences
7) You have the right to change your mind; even at the last minute
8) You have the right to be respected and request that others change their behavior if they are infringing on your rights
9) You have the right to stop and take time to think before acting
10) You have the right to choose whether or not to get involved

Having rights does not mean that you can abuse them nor does it mean that you have to remind someone of your rights daily. The goal is to understand who you are and leverage your rights to reach your goals. Use the effective communication skills that you have learned in previous modules to openly express what your goals are, to ask for assistance in achieving them, and to remove barriers when required to guarantee that your needs are met.

When to assert yourself

As we discussed earlier, not every situation calls for assertion. Understanding when and how to assert yourself can be confusing. Here are a few examples of when assertion is justified:

When opportunities arise

Opportunities are available all of the time. The chance to choose a college, switch jobs, buy a car or go on vacation can be very exciting. Moving too quickly can cause you to make the wrong decision. When opportunities arise, remember regardless of how tantalizing the offer is or how pushy the person pitching the opportunity can be, you still have the right to stop and take time to think prior to making a decision. Perform your due diligence and do your homework. Review the issue or purchase carefully. Talk to people who have purchased or have taken advantage of the opportunity before and then decide on a course of action and act accordingly. Never feel pressured or hurried to make a decision. Choose the option that is best for you, even if the decision is to not act at all.

When the need arises to refuse a request

There will be times that others will ask you to do something that you do not agree with. Whether it is to loan them money, clothing or participate in an activity that you do not value; you have the right to refuse their requests. The best way to refuse is to:

1) State your position by giving them the answer. Example: "NO"
2) Decide whether your response needs an explanation. If you deem that an explanation is necessary, tell them why you gave that answer.
3) Be empathetic and let the person know that you understood their request. Example: "I am sorry to hear that. I am unable to grant your request."

4) Provide an alternative if one exists.
5) Restate your position and hold firm, change the subject or simply walk away.

Some people will have to hear your answer several times before they begin to accept it. Do not allow their persistence to frustrate you. Instead, focus on maintaining your position and practice often.

When you need to make a request and assert your rights

From time to time you will have to ask a question to gain information or to request additional resources. In either case you will need to:

1) State the problem or situation that will need to change.
2) Boldly make your request to correct the shortfall or change the situation.
3) Be prepared to support and defend your request when necessary.

Consider the following as an example, "Jill, I left my purse at home and I don't have any money. Could I borrow 5 bucks for lunch? I will reimburse you when we get back home.

When you have to express your feelings

Tell the other person how you feel and how you think. Resist the urge to be vague. Be direct, open and honest. Tell the person how the situation affects you personally. Use the following sentence construction "I feel __ when you __." Use statements like "I feel that I cannot trust you when you continue to lie." Remember being assertive means that you express yourself without being malicious.

When coping with criticism (dealing with haters)

People will attempt to use criticism to deter and distract you from completing a task or reaching your goals. This form of criticism is a form of manipulation because the goal is not to help you improve but to get you to do what they want you to do. When it is apparent that the goal of the criticism is to manipulate you, verbally disarm the other person by using one of the following techniques:

1) Ask open-ended questions to assess what they are really attempting to get you to do or what they are upset about. Use questions like: "What about my behavior is wrong?" or "What about not wanting to buy anything means I am cheap?
2) Agree with what the accuser is saying "I do that sometimes don't I?"
3) Accept what the accuser is saying "I never take your good qualities into account."

All three techniques can be used in combination to identify the root cause of the issue. Once you find out what the root of the issue is, address it. Be careful and do not use conjunctions like "however" or "but" after agreeing with or accepting what the other person is saying. "But" and "however" nullify what is said before them and allows the listener to disregard what you are saying. Once you address the issue, clarify and restate your position.

Barriers to being assertive

Now that you understand a little more about what

assertiveness is and when to utilize it, we are going to take a look at why some people choose not to be assertive. Most people are apprehensive about being assertive because they lack the confidence in their own abilities to achieve the results they expect or are worried about the consequences of a resulting confrontation (Smith, 1975). They feel that speaking their mind will ruin a relationship. Most people do not want to start an argument, cause a scene or offend the other person. They also may feel that other people's rights and feelings are more important. So, they tell themselves that the issue is "no big deal." Your thoughts, feelings and emotions are just as important as someone else's. The best person to speak for you, is you. You are the only one who knows how you really feel; have the courage to positively express it. Be consistent and persistent. Practice often. You will find that you will get more respect by standing up for what you believe, than conforming for popularity.

Tips for being assertive

- Avoid shouting, trying to talk over the other person, and assigning blame. Instead, understand your rights and use effective communication skills to broker a solution.
- Have a confident demeanor. Try to show that you are confident, even if you are nervous or uncertain.
- Keep your shoulders squared and your chin up. Even if you are confused, you can be confident.
- Look people in the eye. This can be hard for people who are naturally nervous or timid, but it shows people that you don't intend to be brushed off.
- Use a clear, calm voice. You don't need to be loud, but do make yourself heard.

- Make sure your gestures, facial expressions and body language matches your message.
- Know what you want, it makes it easier for others to follow you when you are decisive.
- Once you have made a decision, stick to it. Do not be afraid to restate your position. Be firm but respectful.

Advantages to Being Assertive

If you use the tools discussed in this chapter, you will notice that you have a better chance of getting what you want. You will be less likely to be taken advantage of. You will be less likely to suffer from increased anxiety from having to resolve conflict. You will have the personal satisfaction in knowing you handled the issues and situations correctly. You will improve your self-esteem through a better sense of personal honesty. Most of all, you will identify the proper time to assert yourself, have the courage to seize opportunities, overcome your personal struggle and become a consistent winner.

QUESTIONNAIRE

Answer the following questions:

1) What is the difference between being aggressive and being assertive?

_____
_____
_____
_____

2) Name 3 rights that an assertive person has?

_____
_____
_____

3) When should you be assertive?

_____
_____
_____
_____

4) What are some of the barriers to being assertive?

_____
_____
_____
_____

5) What are some of the advantages of being assertive?

_____

_____

_____

_____

Section 14: Leading Others

Good leaders are made not born. If you are passionate and determined, you can become an effective leader. Good leaders develop through a continuing cycle of assessing self-capability, taking advantage of educational opportunities, reviewing preparation, seeking guidance and documenting experiences. Leadership is a process by which a person influences others to reach goals and coaches in a way that makes the effort to reach the goal more organized and sound. Leaders carry out this process by applying their leadership traits, such as beliefs, values, ethics, character, knowledge and skills.

Concept of Leadership

What makes a person want to follow a leader?

<u>People want to be guided by those they respect</u>. To gain respect, a leader must have sound principles and integrity. The leader must have the capability and willingness to behave in a manner that is consistent with the established principles set for the group (Vieira, 2005). It is vital that the leader be fair and just with correcting issues and dealing with challenges of authority.

<u>People want to be guided by those who have a clear sense of direction.</u> A sense of direction is achieved by conveying a strong vision of the future. It is the ability to develop and implement a plan to move forward. It is also the skill to make keen and decisive decisions (Vieira, 2005).

According to former U.S. President, Dwight D. Eisenhower, "Leadership is the art of getting someone to do something you want done because he or she wants to do it!" (Damiani, 1998, p.1).

As you function in a purpose driven, goal confident and goal determined manner you will attract others to you.

<u>People want to be guided by those who have a track record for overcoming obstacles.</u> The leader must be known for outstanding problem-solving skills. People want to follow someone who is capable of persevering in high pressure situations. The leader must have a reputation for being able to snatch triumph from certain defeat.

Let us examine leadership from another perspective. Read the following three situations in which formal leadership is required. As you examine each situation carefully think about qualities you would like to see in a leader.

1. You are at a block club meeting. The residents are disagreeing about whether the community park that has open basketball should be open after 9:00 p.m. during the weekdays. Tempers are very short on both sides. What are the two most important qualities you want in the chairperson of the meeting?

_____

_____

2. You are on the varsity basketball team with one year to play. You are happy with your basketball skills, but your team, on the other hand, is not doing too well. Many of the players on your team are complaining about the extra practices the coach has added. Your goal is to gain a scholarship to attend college. You have been on the honor roll the last 3 years and will need financial aid. What are the most important qualities you want in your coach?

_____

_____

_____

3. You are flying to Florida for some much needed rest and relaxation. You notice there is more turbulence than normal. People are beginning to panic. What are the two most important qualities you want to see in the pilot?

_____

_____

_____

As a leader you must be many things to many people. Often times, different situations, such as the ones you have read, call for a leader to respond instantly. As a good leader, you have to develop techniques for responding appropriately to the needs of the situation and the needs and expectations of those involved. Continue to build upon your skills, qualities and abilities as a leader to attract and lead others.

Simply put, leadership is influencing the group to accomplish a mutually agreed-upon goal while advancing the group's integrity and morale.

In the language of an eleven-year old, it's "getting the job done and keeping the group together."

The group remains in existence only as long as these two needs are being fulfilled. Being a leader is not the same as being the boss. The following poem says it well:

The Leader
The boss drives group members; the leader coaches them.
The boss depends upon authority; the leader on good will.
The boss inspires fear; the leader inspires enthusiasm.
The boss says "I"; the leader says "we."
The boss assigns the task, the leader sets the pace.
The boss says, "Get there on time"; the leader gets there ahead of time.
The boss fixes the blame for the breakdown; the leader fixes the breakdown.
The boss knows how it is done; the leader shows how.
The boss makes work drudgery; the leader makes it a game.
The boss says, "Go"; the leader says, "Let's go."
 --Author unknown

Authority and Power
What would life be like if there was no one who had the capability to hold us accountable for our actions? For a while, it would seem "cool" to do whatever you wanted to do. Soon you would realize that everyone else would be doing whatever they wanted as well. Most of us would agree that life, as we know it, would be chaotic. Everyone would have the ability to do whatever they pleased, whenever they pleased. Several rights and civil liberties would be violated, several crimes would be committed and many emotional, physical and psychological scars would be developed.

Thankfully, we live in a society that is governed by rules that protect its citizens from chaos. The rules are enforced by several specialized groups that have been given the power to maintain stability. These specialized groups include families, schools, police agencies, religious affiliations and courts. We are held accountable by those who possess certain rights because of the positions of leadership they hold within the specialized group. These positions may include parents, teachers, officers, priests and judges. Each has the power to influence or command thought, opinion or behavior. This power is called authority.

As a leader, how are you using your influence of authority and power?

The Responsibility of Authority

As mentioned above, authority is necessary and important because it helps maintain order in our society, in our families and in our schools. People in positions of authority have the responsibility to use their influence justly. To abuse their power puts the whole system at risk because authority is only as good as those who respect it. Think about it. In politics for example, if the people, who are subject to a leader lose respect for that leader, the leader is systematically removed from office. In situations where the police have lost the respect of the community, the community takes justice into its own hands. Likewise, if parents are not respected, they lose control of their children.

To combat the possibility of losing power, because of insecurity, or out of boldness, some leaders hide behind their positions and use their power or status as a platform to benefit their own agendas. This type of leader may be categorized as the "Discourager" from Chapter 1. This leader may lack their own personal power and have issues with character. If you read the newspapers or surf the internet, you will find they are full of examples of people misusing their positions of authority. In those situations, the people in authority are certainly not automatically worthy of more respect than anyone else!

When you are subject to this leadership type, you may still be obligated to perform tasks imposed out of respect for the position. But remember:

<u>Leaders do not have the right to abuse their authority.</u> You do not have to be disrespected, forced to go against your core values or support issues you do not believe in just because someone has been given authority over you. In situations like these, you will need to confide in a person you can trust. This person can be a mentor, a teacher or a trustworthy relative.

<u>Leaders have been given power only to perform a service.</u> Understand that people in authority have been given certain powers and benefits because they have a service to perform. You are one of the people they provide a service to. They have an obligation to make the right decisions concerning you, your development, your goals or your safety. Hold them accountable for the decisions they make. Learn from their poor examples of leadership.

As you become a better leader, you will gain influence through the trust and respect of others. Understand that this trust and respect comes from your outward ability to inwardly see the bigger picture and take the appropriate action. Do not misuse your level of influence. Instead, develop your own sense of natural authority. You can do this by encouraging a sense of pride, dignity, independence and achievement in yourself, first. Then, work on the same traits in the people who look to you for leadership (Maxwell, 1999).

Developing Leadership Traits

"When people make a decision (either consciously or unconsciously) to follow your leadership, they do it primarily because of one of two things: your character or your skills. They want to know if you are the kind of person they want to follow and if you have the skills to take them further. Yes, there are other variables, but these are the bulk of the matter. Now we're going to focus on the kind of character that causes people to follow your leadership" (Widener, n.d. para. 1).

Integrity

Integrity is the notion that you do what you say you will. You are faithful and dependable. People can rely on you because you keep your promises. The only thing that will prohibit others from following you is lack of trust. It is the feeling of uncertainty in your ability to actually take them where you say you will. Are you known as a person of integrity? If so, you will become an extraordinary leader!

Optimistic

People don't want to follow others who think the future is bleak! They want to follow those who can see light at the end of the tunnel, can get others to believe that light exists and that they can get them there! If you see the cup as half empty, you are a pessimist and will have to change your thoughts and attitude about the situation in order to be a good leader. Seeing the glass as half full places you are on your way to becoming an optimist. If you see it as totally full -- half air and half water and can convince others of the same, you are well on your way to being a good leader.

Embrace Change

Leaders are the ones who will see the need for change and are willing to embrace it. Followers typically, will have no desire to move or see the need to change. Leaders need to see the benefits of change, effectively communicate them to followers, and encourage the followers to change. A fish that stays in the same aquarium will grow to a point and stop. Eventually, its environment stunts its growth. In the same manner, without change you will become stagnant, and you will never grow! Are you known as a person who embraces change?

Risk Taker

Whenever we try something new, we are taking a risk. Risk is part of growing and it is imperative to our development. Most people are skeptical of taking risk. A major component of leadership is the ability to calculate the risk and understand both the rewards and the consequences of their decisions. Once a decision is made, they confidently communicate the vision to the followers. The plan is implemented and the organization gains from the experience. Are you known as a person who is willing to take risks?

Tenacious

Lack of leadership causes the follower to quit when the going gets tough. After two or three tries, their motto becomes, "If at first you don't succeed, give up and try something else." Conversely, leaders know what good lies beyond the obstacle and they will go and get it. Leaders press forward, forge a trail and bring others with them! Are you known as a person who is tenacious? Learn to be persistent (Widener, n.d.).

Catalytic

A leader is ultimately one who provides the spark to light others passions. They are able to get others out of their comfort zone and on toward the goal! They can raise the zeal, enthusiasm and the ACTION of those who would follow. Are you known as a catalyst? Become a catalyst and start a chain reaction (Widener, n.d.).

Dedicated/Committed

Followers want people who are more devoted and committed to the team and the stated goal more than they are. At the first sign of unfaithfulness, followers lose faith and scatter. As we stated earlier in this chapter, followers follow those who will stick it out because they see how significant the task is in relation to the overall goal. Are you known as a person who is committed and devoted to the goal? Devote yourself to becoming dedicated to the team (Widener, n.d.).

How to develop your personal growth plan using the 5-step improvement process

1) Assess your current state. Perform a self-assessment. Take an inventory of your dreams, ambitions, goals and aspirations. Then, take a look at your daily activities and see if they are consistent with reaching your goals.

2) Identify opportunities for improvement. Review your self-assessment. Then, identify the few key areas in your life that you would like to improve and develop. These goals should deal with character growth or the development of personal skills. Think about: Which key areas will you need to improve in to be successful? Which tasks will have the greatest impact on your development? Develop a system of prioritization.

3) Develop an action plan. Review your opportunities for improvement and use the following tools to develop an action plan. Prioritize plan tasks based on their relative impact on your goal.

a) **Brainstorm.** Come up with ideas on how you may address your area for opportunity and decide on the most appropriate tasks.

b) **Look for resources in these areas.** List the resources that you may need to find that will assist you in developing in each of the areas you have identified.

   i) Resources may include books, websites, blogs, tapes, seminars or training to attend.

   ii) List the resources that you will use to help you in your personal growth.

   iii) Identify the costs associated with gaining additional resources. Put a plan in place to gain the identified resources.

c) **Find mentors and build relationships with other growing people.** This is one of the most under-valued areas of personal development. Relationships with experienced and wise people will help you to grow faster than any other medium. Wisdom comes with experience and you can benefit from the experiences of someone who has gone where you want to go. They can help you avoid some of the pitfalls associated with your growth plan.

   i) **Look for area experts.** Look for mentors who are proficient in each of the key areas identified to support and guide you as you develop.

    ii) **Multiple mentors are usually better than one.** This is true because it is unlikely you'll be able to find a single person to assist you in all your key areas. List the potential mentors and growing people that you are going to actively develop a relationship with.

4) Implement your plan of attack. Once you have a plan, it is time to put it in action.
- a. **Set aside an hour a day dedicated to your personal development.** You will need to create an hour each day to implement your growth plan. This is a regular time set aside to focus on developing the areas identified, used for reading, writing and making additional contacts (if needed).
- b. **Attempt to work on your growth plan in the same spot.** Attempting to work on your growth plan in the same spot will re-enforce the habit of working on your development each day.

5) Review and Assess!!! Reflect on how successful you were in accomplishing your goals. What lessons can you learn from this experience that will aid you in planning for future goals?

Develop your personal growth plan, make it a visual poster and hang it up where you can see it daily. Then create a daily habit of spending an hour dedicated to reaching your personal development goals.

GAME ON: Tools and Strategies for Living on Purpose

QUESTIONNAIRE

Answer the following questions:

1. What are the primary reasons why people choose to follow some leaders and not others?

_____
_____
_____

2. How is a leader different from someone who just bosses people around?

_____
_____
_____

3. Why are power and authority important?

_____
_____
_____

4. What responsibilities do all leaders have?

_____
_____
_____

5. Which leadership traits do you currently have? Which traits will you have to develop?

_____
_____

References

10 tips to change your attitude today. (2011, December). Retrieved from http://www.1quote-in.

An introduction to nonverbal communication. (2012, March 20). Retrieved from http://www.connectrecruitment.co.nz/blog/article

Assertiveness (n.d.). Retrieved from http://hiphoptalks.com.

Benson, J. & Haith, M. (2009). *Social and emotional development in infancy and early childhood* [chart]. San Diego, CA: Academic Press.

Bergstrom, C. (2002). *A story of loss and comfort I know this is what I'm supposed to do.* Maitland, FL: Xulon Press.

Bower, S. (1991). *Asserting yourself: A practical guide for positive change.* Boston, MA: Da Capo Press.

Chapman, G. (1997). *The five love languages of children.* Chicago, IL: Northfield Publishing.

Conformity. (2006). Retrieved from www.bookrags.com.

Damiani, A. (1998). *Creative leadership: Mining the gold in your workforce.* Boca Raton, FL: CRC Press.

Difficult troubled teens. (n.d.) *Center for adolescent recovering and education.* Retrieved from www.receivetroubleteens.com.

Gabler, N. (2007). *Walt Disney the triumph of the American imagination.* New York, NY: Random House.

Hill, N. (1990). *Think and grow rich.* New York, NY: Random House.

Hunter, J. (2013). *Mormons and popular culture: The global influence of an American phenomenon.* Santa Barbara, CA: ABC-CLIO.

Kimbro, D. (1991). *Think and grow rich: A black choice.* New York, NY: Random House.

Life. (n.d.). Volume 9.

Maxwell, J. (2009). *How successful people think: Change your thinking, change your life*. New York, NY: Center Street Publishing.

Maxwell, J. (1999). *The 21 irrefutable laws of leadership: Follow them and they will follow you*. Nashville, TN: Thomas Nelson, Inc.

Mussieux, P. (n.d.). *Motivation vs. inspiration*. Retrieved from http://www.evancarmichael.com.

O'Brien, S. (Narrator). (2009). Black in America II. [Television]. New York, NY: CNN.

Oprah and Bill Gates have mentors. Do you? (March, 2011). Retrieved from http://www.theworkbuzz.com.

Positive self-esteem. (n.d.) *Mountain state centers for independent living*. Retrieved from www.mtstcil.org.

Prinstein, M. & Dodge, K. (2005) *Understanding peer influence in children and adolescents*. New York, NY: Guilford Press.

"Remember your good qualities [Chart]". (2004) *Vitiligo friends*. Retrieved from www.vitiligocover.com.

Roller coaster history ride designers. (n.d.). Retrieved from http://www.ultimaterollercoaster.com.

Scott, E. (n.d.) Reduce stress with increased assertiveness. *Townsville business women's network*.Retrieved from www.businesswomen.com.

Smith, M. (1975).*When I say no, I feel guilty*. New York, NY: Bantam Books.

Smith, M. (2000). *When I say no, I feel guilty, vol. II, for managers and executives*. A Train Press.

"Take the test [chart]". Retrieved from http://www.mtstcil.org/skills/image-test.

The nine basic human needs. (1997, June). Retrieved from http://www.itstime.com.
True story of Tyler Perry. (2011, June 16). *Entrepreneur voices.* Retrieved from http://www.entrepreneurvoices.com.
U.S. Congress, Office of Technology Assessment. (1990, January). *Critical connections: communication for the future.* U.S. Government Printing Office.
Vieira, W. (2005). *Manager to CEO wisdom for survival and success.* Thousand Oaks, CA: Sage Publications.
Widener, C. (n.d.). Top 7 character traits of extra ordinary leaders. *Christopher M. Knight's top 7 business.* Retrieved from http://top7business.com.
Ziglar, Z. (2006). *Better than good: Creating a life you can't wait to live.* New York, NY: Thomas Nelson Inc.
Ziglar, Z. (1985). *Raising positive kids in a negative world.* New York, NY: Thomas Nelson Inc.
Ziglar, Z. (2006). *See you at the top.* New York, NY: G P Putnam's Sons.

Articles and Case Studies

1. Sharpe, Tom; Balderson, Daniel. "The Effects of Personal Accountability and Personal Responsibility Instruction on Select Off-Task and Positive Social Behaviors." Journal of Teaching in Physical Education, vol 24. Jan 2005: p66-87.

2. Furterer, Sandra, "Sunshine High School Discipline Process Improvement – A Lean Six Sigma Case Study." Lean Six Sigma in Service: Applications and Case Studies . 2009. Florida: Taylor and Franchise Group. p.73-153.

a. Russell, Christina; Mielke, Monica; Reisner, Elizabeth. "Evidence of Program Quality and Youth Outcomes in the DYCD Out-of-School Time Initiative: Report on the Initiative's First Three Years. September 2009. Wallace White Spaces

Disclaimers

Names, characters, places, and incidents are either products of the author's ideas or are used fictitiously. Any resemblance to actual events, locales, or persons, living or dead, is purely coincidental.

Sensible Business Consulting Group LLC makes no warranty, either expressed or implied, including but not limited to any implied warranties of merchantability and fitness for a particular purpose, regarding any programs or book materials and makes such materials available solely on an "as is" basis.

In no event shall Sensible Business Consulting Group LLC, Novi, Michigan, be liable to anyone for special, collateral, incidental or consequential damages in connection with or arising out of the purchase or use of these materials, and the sole and exclusive liability of Sensible Business Consulting Group LLC, Novi, Michigan, regardless of the form of action, shall not exceed the purchase price of this book. Moreover, Sensible Business Consulting Group LLC, Novi, Michigan, shall not be liable for any claim whatsoever against the use of these materials by any other party.

 Dr. Joseph E. Kimbrough, renowned speaker, educator, engineer, author, activist and entrepreneur delivers high energy messages that engage, empower, equip, elevate and encourage businesses, communities, and educational institutes to improve their bottom line.

After overcoming many obstacles such as living in the Foster Care System, Kimbrough went on to obtain a Master of Science degree in both Manufacturing and Engineering Management from Eastern Michigan University and recently obtained his Doctorate of Education in Leadership and Management from St. Thomas University, Miami, FL. Kimbrough has held various positions from College Professor to Senior Corporate Quality Director. He has earned both his Lean 6-Sigma Master Black Belt and Executive Leadership Coaching certification from Lawrence Technological University, Southfield MI.

In 2009, Kimbrough became the founder and director of Sensible Business Consulting Group, LLC and Sensible Business Career and Training Institute. Kimbrough has over 20 years of extensive experience in various aspects of product engineering, manufacturing, education, quality and continuous improvement as well as executive coaching, directing organizational change initiatives, leadership and team development, workforce development and strategic planning.

His zeal and passion for life fuels his desire to be an inspiration to everyone he encounters. As a philanthropist his desire is to help others achieve their DREAMS and bring RESTORATION within the community. He sits on several boards and currently serves as the Chair of Robichaud Academy of Engineering. In addition, he served as the Leadership Institute Dean and Director of Family Life and Empowerment at Triumph Church, which according to Outreach Magazine is the fastest growing church in the United States with over 20,000 members.

Kimbrough has been featured in magazines, on television and nationwide radio including, but not limited to: NBC, WRDT, WMUZ, CTN, TV33 WHPR, City Talk Magazine, Detroit News, Observer and Eccentric Newspapers. He currently has a weekly radio segment, called "GAME ON Wednesday" on WPZR.

Dr. Kimbrough can be reached for consultations, motivational/public speaking, conducting workshops, book-signings or training sessions - log on to:

www.gameondr.com

About Sensible Business Consulting Group, LLC

Sensible Business Consulting Group (SBCG) LLC is a North American provider of comprehensive quality solutions such as training and consulting services. We are a diverse company with a variety of tools that are applicable to every industry. SBCG specializes in providing quality services in career and leadership development, quality improvement of products or processes in product engineering, manufacturing, healthcare and services industries utilizing Lean, Six-Sigma and Total Quality Management (TQM) tools . We are committed to building leadership in industry and the community - one person, one process at a time. Through our diverse affiliations, skillful consultants, and experienced facilitators, we are poised to help foster positive attitudes and productivity amongst our clients. Our process focuses on creating a positive self-image through developing interpersonal skills, communication, goal setting, and achievement.

For more information about additional resources and training materials, log on to www.sensiblebusiness.org

CPSIA information can be obtained
at www.ICGtesting.com
Printed in the USA
FFOW04n1307110215
11004FF